SUNDAY ADELAJA

HOW TO
REGAIN YOUR
LOST YEARS

Sunday Adelaja

HOW TO REGAIN YOUR LOST YEARS

©2017 Sunday Adelaja

Edited by Adaora I. Anisiobi (M. pharm.)

ISBN 978-1-908040-61-9

Cover design by Oleksandr Bondaruk

Interior design by Oleksandr Bondaruk

CONTENTS

INTRODUCTION

I was conducting an online training for my mentees recently on time management and the principles of time conversion. They were amazed at my teachings but disheartened because they realized they had lost many years of their lives due to their ignorance.

Majority expressed concern over their poor time management skills and began to ask if there was a remedy to their dilemma. Almost all of them admitted being guilty of not appreciating time but rather wasting it through bad habits which includes excessive indulgence in social media, TV and movies, excessive social activities etc.

Some expressed their ignorance of the importance of discovering the purpose of God for their lives and fulfilling it instead of their personal agenda. They admitted that they were not pursuing God's plans in their career but are merely working to make ends meet. They wondered if it were possible to switch to their divine career at their age seeing they have gone too far down the wrong road.

I heard sad stories of how some were trapped in the wrong career just to satisfy the selfish desires of their parents, family members and employers and a lot of years have gone by. Several talked about talents and gifts they never developed because they felt they could not generate enough money to feed them and pay their bills much less make them rich.

The huge number of responses prompted me to not only teach them about ways to salvage their lost years but also to write this book so as to help more people out there who find themselves in the same predicament. This book is a result of not merely the pleas of my mentees but also those of a number of people I have met in my work as a pastor and life coach.

Life is about discovering the purpose of God for our lives and living to fulfill it. And when people are ignorant of this fundamental truth, they live unfulfilled lives. I have met a lot of people who are in the wrong jobs. Their job is a burden and they moan on Mondays and celebrate when Friday arrives. They spend forty or more hours of their lives every week doing something they do not enjoy simply to make ends meet. Although their hearts are in another career, their hands are slaving away at their current jobs. That's why there are teachers doing construction work, dentists working as bank executives and musicians taking care of patients in the hospitals.

But God has a purpose for every human being born in this world. He created us with gifts and talents and expects us to develop them and use them to make life better for both us and others. God has also ordained our prosperity to be in the area of our calling or purpose therefore it is imperative for everyone to discover their purpose and set goals on how to accomplish it. Anything done outside the purpose of God will ultimately lead to an unfulfilled life.

Although for many, a lot of water has gone under the bridge, yet with the strategies which I have outlined in this book, it is possible to turn around and proceed in the right direction to fulfill their purpose.

This process starts with developing a keen sense of appreciation of the treasure called time. Time is our greatest resource. When people are not skillful with time; when they have not learnt to manage and use time, and when they are unable to rule over time, a lot will be lost in their lives.

We understand that time lost can never be regained, but with the strategies discussed in this book, we can boldly step out to fulfill our goals with the remaining time. A lot of people have been able to reclaim their lost years, financially, career-wise and in their personal lives. They serve as an encouragement for others to forge ahead in their desire to live a fulfilled life.

Have you always wanted to write books or be a motivational speaker but you have no idea on how to develop the gift? Or you wanted to be an entrepreneur but too scared to leave the comfort of your *nine to five* job?

It is time to unearth those gifts and talents that are buried inside you and re-awaken those deeply buried passions and develop them into valuable products and services that will enrich your life and those of mankind.

Armed with the proper time management techniques and special qualities that will enable you to maximize your remaining time to the fullest, you can launch out with full confidence to reclaim your lost years and fulfill the purpose of God for your life.

PRACTICAL SUGGESTIONS FOR READING THIS BOOK

THIS BOOK CAN CHANGE YOUR LIFE!

Often, when reading a book, we decide to apply every life lesson we gain. But much more often, after only a few weeks, we have completely forgotten about our intentions. You can have a lot of knowledge in your head, but do not use them or live them. Much of what you will read here will not be something new for you. The question is what you will do with this.

Here are six practical ways to turn your good intentions into at least the good actions:

1. Read this book several times

Often stop reading the book to reflect on its content. Ask yourself, how and when you can apply a particular recommendation. After a detailed study of the book, re-read it every month, giving it a few hours. This book should become a permanent fixture on your desk.

2. Read aloud

Reading aloud helps to release in your life the power that stands behind every word. It is not only important that every word be seen, but also that every word be heard. The spoken word has a wave nature, and therefore, when it sounds, it has a changing effect on all surrounding objects and subjects. Thus, words have meaning. Do not neglect the power of words! Don't allow to pass you by, the force that can literally physically begin to change your life and its circumstances!

3. Underline and make notes

Reading this book, keep a pen or a text divider (markers). Emphasise individual lines of text and paragraphs — this simple action will triple your ability to remember. On the margins of the book, record your thoughts and make notes — let this book be your book. Underlining makes the book much more interesting and in the future helps to quickly see it again.

4. Again and again, re-read the underlined parts

By underlining and annotation, you can quickly view the most important issues and fragments of this book. To read the book and get the result you want, you have to view it as often as possible. Let the selected fragments inspire you to improve your life. As humans, we have an amazing ability to forget. The only way to keep the necessary information in memory is to return to it again and again.

5. Immediately apply the principles learned

Applying what is learned allows us to better understand and remember what is heard. It is impossible to teach a man anything; he can only learn. This means that learning is an active process. Most of all, we learn best through practice. If you want to master the principles outlined in this book, use them as often as possible and whenever possible. If you will not practice, you will quickly forget. Only what is applied in practice, remains in memory.

6. Give priority to what you learn

Select from one to three points, to start with. Start to constantly apply them until they become a habit. Practical benefits that you will derive from this book can become your habit only as a result of its constant repetition. Only in this way will you grow to use it unconsciously.

At the end of each Chapter you will find the Golden nuggets — an accumulation of all the important ideas expressed throughout the Chapter. You will also see tests against which you can evaluate yourself and your skills, and Practical exercises that will help you to translate what you've read into life. They are not just for reading. To help you get the maximum results and benefits from the practical tasks, we strongly recommend you perform them within 24 hours, otherwise you will be overtaken by vanity; you will be once again distanced from your destiny, and those changes you expect in your life will not happen.

In my long experience with people I know usually people do a similar job for the sake of appearances. But you are not in school, where you get away with different kinds of replies. We are talking about your life, from the fulfillment of these buildings depends on how much your life will change. Therefore, I urge you to take the tasks seriously, as they are not for the author of the book, but for you. To perform the tasks, it is desirable to find a quiet place where no one will be able to interfere with you. Perhaps it will be a time when no one is home, or the night when everyone is asleep, and nobody will disturb you.

Be sure to reflect on the previous Chapter, over all the items which you emphasized for yourself; remember your choices and write down your next steps. Don't forget to set a specific time frame to determine the restrictions that you

will impose on yourself. This will help you not to postpone

the planned steps to change your life and put them "on

the back burner." Find someone to whom you could be ac-

countable for your decisions, who could recall, or partner

with you to work on yourself.

Write down the date you start reading this book. Let that

specified date be for you the beginning of a turning point

in your life!

CHAPTER 1

CAN I REGAIN MY LOST YEARS?

Many people all over the world ask the silent question *"Can I regain my lost years?"*

I met a lady in the store a few years ago. She was a cashier but her passion was to be a nurse. She was 43 years old. She had so much passion for taking care of the sick that it was obvious she would make a great nurse. She told me her story; she had no one to support her education so she dropped out of school and resorted to menial jobs to take care of herself. She had two kids out of wedlock, became a single mom and her financial situation worsened. Then she took up several jobs in order to cater for her babies and herself. Over those years she gave up on her dreams and having secured a stable job as a cashier in a good company, she settled completely. Although her babies were grown, she had no intention of reviving her passion, because according to her, "it was too late." This is because she did not know the principles of reclaiming lost years.

A gentleman came to me after church service recently. He wanted to be an entrepreneur but had not taken a step towards his dream and was in his fifties. He believed it was too late to leave the comfort of his job and venture into the unknown waters of entrepreneurship. He explained that he had put in so much energy and time in his current job and had risen to an enviable position but still felt unfulfilled. He had chosen to continue with his job, retire later and live off his retirement benefits.

The truth is that a lot of people have lost many years of their lives. They are not living the life they desired to live. People usually start off with so many dreams and visions but as life progresses, most of their dreams are overtaken by life itself. A lot of people are hunted by the fact that their lives are polar opposites of their life's purpose. While some who are not really sure of what their purpose is, are simply living in regret of missed opportunities, procrastinated dreams and failed aspirations that they wonder "Can anything be done? Is it possible to make up for the time lost?"

People are losing precious hours of their life doing something that is outside of their purpose and passion. These people feel trapped in their current jobs and it is hard for them to turn around and pursue their dreams because it seems 'too late'. Most people have given up hopes of ever living their dreams again. Some, however still nurse a little hope and they are the ones asking, "Can I regain my lost years?"

Yes, there are lots of reasons for it but people have found themselves along pathways they did not choose and have continued along such paths for such a long time that they wonder if it is possible to chart their own course in life. They are living the life they unconsciously chose and not the one chosen by their creator.

Some people on the other hand lost many years of their lives as a result of procrastination. They lacked the ability to rule over their time and now they are haunted by all the dreams they procrastinated on, "Oh, Someday, I will get that education; Someday, I will write a book." They pushed their dreams and aspirations to a non-existent place called "*someday*" hoping that someday will arrive, only to wake up one day and see the grey hairs, weak muscles, dim eyesight, the tell-tale signs of old age. That's when it dawned on them that "someday" may never arrive.

It could be getting a post-graduate degree. Although they understood the importance of a higher degree in climbing the corporate ladder yet they procrastinated. And now they wonder if it is possible to achieve their dreams again.

Another area where a lot of people have lost time is in the area of finances. I know of a lot of people who had this particular problem. They did not learn the laws of money on time and lived in ignorance of how wealth is built. Some have attended my seminars and after hearing me teach about the Laws of Money, they usually ask if it still possible for them to achieve financial freedom at their age.

Yet still, some have lost so many years of their lives due to failures and set-backs. In life, we encounter crisis and adversity that rob us of our valuable resources and investments accumulated over many years. Crises are a part of life's equation. As a matter of fact, it is understood that in some Asian culture, the word *crisis* is non-existent in their vocabulary; instead it is replaced by the word *opportunity*.

Some lost businesses and financial investments they spent years building. We remember the major economic meltdown of 2008 which affected many countries in the world. People lost in one year, what they built over many years. Their labor of many years disappeared in an instant.

According to The Pew Charitable Trust report on The Impact of the September 2008 Economic Collapse, *'U.S. households lost on average nearly $5,800 in income due to reduced economic growth during the acute stage of the financial crisis from September 2008 through the end of 2009. Also, the combined peak loss from declining stock and home values totalled nearly $100,000, on average per U.S. household, during the July 2008 to March 2009 period.'*[1]

Some people have lost all their life savings in a natural disaster. Hurricanes, floods and fire outbreaks has rendered many people homeless and bereft of all their possessions. Properties, Homes, businesses and other valuables are lost and it is worst in countries where properties are not insured. These are not mere properties; they were acquired over years so their loss is equal to loss of time.

The impact of Hurricane Katrina which hit the shores of the United States on August 29, 2005 was estimated at $200 billion. The storm which left about 80% of the city flooded led the Congress to approve 62,3 billion for emergency responses. The Hurricane Katrina is the most economically costly hurricane to ever strike the shores of the US.[2]

So what about you? Have you lost time in any area of your life? Do you have any regrets about how you managed your time? Are you actively pursuing your life's purpose or are you caught up in that web of procrastination waiting for someday to pursue your dreams, develop your talents, start saving or become financially independent?

The truth remains that a lot of people have lost a lot of time but some are mourning the loss of their years by living in regret. Regret is not the solution to the problem rather it compounds it. Regret incapacitates and blinds one from seeing opportunities and taking any step towards their dreams and so many die, without achieving their dreams. No wonder the world famous Dr. Myles Munroe often said that the richest place on earth is the cemetery because therein lies a lot of unutilized gifts, talents and potentials. Poems unwritten, songs unsung, inventions undiscovered, because having lost time, most have concluded that it is lost forever.

So the question remains, *"Can I regain my lost years?"*

Well, I bring hope and good news to you today. Yes, you can regain your lost years! There are people who have re-claimed their lost years, in various aspects of their lives. For some it was their financial years, others set out to pur-sue their divine purpose and they ended up successful and fulfilled. I have helped many to regain their lost years. The cashier I mentioned who had given up on her dreams of becoming a nurse is currently a licensed nurse. She took my advice and worked with the instructions I will discuss in this book. She is making more money than before and is enjoying her nursing career. She is happy and feels fulfilled. The older gentleman has also stepped out into the field of entrepreneurship. His company is flourishing and he has over fifty people in his payroll. He is amazed at his progress and wishes he had met me earlier.

These are just a few. A lot of my church members are doing exploits in their old age. We have a Seventy-year-old man doing his PhD program and Sixty-year-old embarking on huge projects and starting churches in foreign nations. There are some mothers in my church who are pastors of large congregations, PhD students, CEOs of multi-million dollar companies while taking care of their families simultaneously. They have all learnt to maximise their potentials by maximizing their time. Their secret is what I will share with you in this book.

FROM BANKRUPCY TO WEALTH

Walt Disney, the famous cartoon creator, filed for bankruptcy in 1920 after one of his main clients filed for bankruptcy.

In the year 1920 Disney formed his first animation company Laugh-O-Gram Studio in Kansas, with the intention of making animated fairy tales. Laugh-O-Gram found a financial backer in New York and Disney began building up his staff of animators. However, the backing firm went broke, and Disney was no longer able to pay his employees or his debts. The company filed bankruptcy and lost Laugh-O-Gram Studios. In 1923 Disney formed a new company with a loan from his parents and his brother. In 1928 he created Mickey Mouse, which took his career to new heights.

In 1937, close to bankruptcy for a second time in his short career, Disney approached the bank for a loan to complete his film. This loan was agreed and Disney was able to fund his staff and studio through to full completion of one of the most notable film releases of all time. Walt Disney was worth $5 billion at the time of his death in 1966.[3]

Donald Trump despite four bankruptcy claims is currently a billionaire and Henry Ford rebuilt his business and died a billionaire.

These men are examples that show you can rebuild a business after experiencing failures and bankruptcy. They didn't abort their dreams of building a great business neither did they live a life of regret; they got up and tried again. Therefore, if you have suffered financial loss, you can regain what you lost. It is rare to find a successful entrepreneur who did not lose a huge part or all of his investments at some point in his career.

LATE BLOOMERS

A late blooming adult is a person who does not discover their talents and abilities until later than normally expected. In other words, these individuals began pursuing their God-given purpose very late in life. Although they started late, they were able to make a success of their lives by achieving their dreams. So if you have not discovered God's purpose for your life or you have been living in procrastination, the stories of these late bloomers will encourage you to take action.

They are found in all fields of life, including art, music, sciences and business. The Bible also tells the stories of some late bloomers. A famous late bloomer is Colonel Harland David Sanders, the founder of a popular Fast Food Restaurant chain called Kentucky Fried Chicken (KFC) in the USA with franchisees worldwide is a good example of a late bloomer who achieved success in business. Before delving into the food business, Sanders worked as a railroad laborer, insurance salesman, and Motel manager. At the age of 40, he started selling fried chicken from his roadside restaurant. But his restaurant closed due to low patronage after another highway was constructed. He developed the concept of restaurant franchisee and at 62 years, the first franchise of his restaurant opened in Utah. The franchise rapidly expanded all over the United States and by 1964, at the age of 74 years, Sanders sold the company for 2 million dollars.[4]

The story of Sanders shows that it is not too late to start the journey to financial freedom. Since he became a millionaire at an old age, you too can! Mr. Sanders according to the story started marketing his franchise concept at the age of 62. It was a new concept at that time, but he persisted and eventually, he succeeded. Therefore, in case you lost all you had in a failed business venture or you are yet to step out, you can borrow a leaf from Mr. Sanders.

The story of Moses in the bible is another example of a late bloomer who found himself in the wrong career. According to the Bible, in Exodus Chapters 2 and 3, Moses was raised in the palace of Pharaoh, the king of Egypt as the son of Pharaoh's daughter. But he wanted to save his fellow Israelites and killed an Egyptian in the process. He was 40 years old. He fled on exile and became a shepherd in a foreign land. The dream of being a deliverer of the Jews was dead and forgotten, but not with God. 40 years later, at the old age of 80, God called him while in the mountains taking care of animals. He was instructed to go back to Egypt and deliver the Israelite. He returned and at 80, he successfully led the Israelites out of bondage.

God does not recognize our age limitations and neither should you. You can get on the path to fulfilling your purpose at any age.

Other late bloomers in arts include Elizabeth Jolley who published her first book at 53 years and proceeded to author 15 other novels and some other short stories. Mary Wesley published her first book at 71 years. She eventually became one of Britain's most successful novelists, selling three million copies of her books, including 10 bestsellers in the last 20 years of her life. At her age, a lot people would be lying in a rocking chair, sipping their tea and waiting for death to come take them. But she set out to fulfill her passion!

Another interesting late bloomer is Anna Mary Robertson Moses, known as Grandma Moses. She started painting at 78 years when the pain of arthritis did not permit her to knit further. She produced over 3,600 paintings with one of them selling for $1,2 million in 2006.

These stories show us that life is not about how early you started but how well you finish your life's purpose A lot of people started late in life but achieved great success whereas, some started early but got distracted along the way and became failures. They failed because they did not pick themselves up afterwards. So despite your age, I want to reassure you that you can still reclaim your lost years, pursue that divine purpose and make something great out of your life.

CONCLUSION

We have established the fact that many people have lost years of their lives especially in the area of fulfilling their divine purpose. Some procrastinated and did not begin the journey whereas some quit after hitting some major obstacles. But we have seen from the lives of some people that it is not too late to start again. The purpose of this book is not just to affirm that it is possible to reclaim your lost years but to show you practical ways to do so.

What I will teach you in this book has helped numerous people whom I have had the privilege of meeting in over two decades of being a pastor. Many of them are doing amazing things and achieving beyond their imaginations despite their ages. So what you will learn have been tested and proven. You too, can fulfill your dreams and passions, achieve greatness, or become financially independent, despite your age.

In the subsequent chapters, I will teach you certain principles, habits, attitudes, patterns and lifestyle adjustments that will enable you fight and recover your time. You will learn to rule over your time and handle it with wisdom. In addition, I will show you how to invest maximum value into every hour of your day.

GOLDEN NUGGETS

- A lot of people have lost a lot of their years by not pursuing their dreams and visions.

- Lost years can be a result of procrastination or failure to get up after experiencing disappointments.

- Yes, you can regain your lost years!

- To regain our lost years, we must be ready to change our negative mindset, attitudes, habits and patterns and imbibe new concepts.

- There are lots of late bloomers who have achieved success despite their old age.

- God does not recognize age limitations in the pursuit of our calling and purpose.

CHAPTER 2

....

TIME, OUR GREATEST TREASURE

It never ceases to amaze me how people trifle with time. Yet it is their greatest treasure. The reason is not far-fetched though. They mismanage time because they have no understanding of the importance and value of time. So first and foremost, we will begin by studying this wonderful treasure called time. By the time we conclude this chapter, your sense of appreciation of time would have soared. You will begin to appreciate every single minute and hour of your day.

THE IMPORTANCE OF TIME

Time is the most valuable resource that God gave mankind. Every human being that is alive is blessed with this wonderful treasure called time. It is given equally as 24 hours per day, so no one can complain of being cheated by the creator. The poor receives 24 hours and the rich also gets 24 hours every day. The difference between both lies in the way they manage their time.

Why is time so important? Why do successful people treasure their time while the unsuccessful people trivialize theirs? Why do Millionaires complain of insufficient time to perform their tasks whereas poor people wonder what to do with their excess time? Hardly do you see a successful person who sits to watch TV for more than one hour, but a lot of broke people live in front of their TV sets. According to Thomas Corley, author of "Rich Habits: The Daily Success Habits Of Wealthy Individuals" 67 percent of rich people only watch TV for one hour or less per day. Also, only 6 percent of the wealthy watch reality shows, while 78 percent of the poor do.[1]

Successful people understand the value of time while unsuccessful ones do not. The successful appreciate every second of their day because they realize the following:

EVERYTHING IS A PRODUCT OF TIME

Time can be converted into tangible or intangible products such as goods and services. Houses, Cars, Movies, Paintings, College Degrees are products of time because time was invested in the process of their production. Everything we see was made out of time.

Using a house for instance, all the people who were involved in the entire process of building the house were paid for their time. The house was built with materials that were manufactured by people who spent time doing so. The house was designed and built by people who were paid hourly or monthly for the time they spent. So when you purchase that house, you are paying for the time that was involved in the production process. You are paying for the time of the architects, builders, engineers and others that built the house.

Intangible products like services e.g. customer service, medical treatment, nursing treatment are products of time because somebody's time, was used to create that service and that person was remunerated in cash for it.

So when you understand that nothing can be made out-side of time, and the more time you have, the more goods and services you can provide, then your attitude towards time will change.

Because successful people understand that the more time you have the more goods and services you can pro-vide, apart from maximizing their time, they also devise ways to multiply their time by using other people's time. This concept will be discussed in Chapter 13.

Life is calibrated in time

Our life is calibrated in time, i.e. years. A 50 year old has spent about 438,000 hours of his life (50 years × 365 days × 24 hours). Therefore to waste one hour of time is to waste an hour of your life. In the words of Charles Darwin; *A man who dares to waste one hour of time has not discovered the value of life."*

This is because life is the sum total of your hours. If you really want to fulfill your life's purpose, then you need to pay attention to each hour of your life because those hours make up your entire life. And that means every passing second and minute of your life matter because they make up your hours and your life. As the seconds are ticking off, your life time is diminishing. As the minutes are going, your life is being spent!

A keen sense of appreciation of this treasure called time is the first step towards regaining our lost years. You must learn to value and treat time like the successful and wise do.

*Teach us to number our days so that we can apply
our hearts to wisdom.*
PSALM 90:12 KJV

This verse from the scriptures shows that wisdom is about how well we manage our time. If you trivialize time, then you will waste your life. But if you value, treasure and prioritize it, then you will maximize it.

Time cannot be stopped

Time cannot be stopped, or placed on hold as you would do to a car or a phone call. So even if you aren't ready for time, it keeps ticking. No wonder they say that *time waits for no man*. It doesn't wait, it flies.

Successful people understand that since no one can stop time, you have to run with it. Therefore, they fight to keep up with time and invest into time.

Imagine that you are in a race and beside you, on the next track is your opponent called time. He doesn't get tired and never stops, so how can you effectively compete with such an opponent?

"You may delay, but time will not." — Benjamin Franklin

Time will never delay, pause or stop for you so it is important to develop good time management skills so as to compete effectively.

Time cannot be stored

We tend to store and preserve our valuables. We can store fresh produce to make them last longer, and bank our precious stones and metals to protect them from thieves etc.

Unfortunately as precious as time is, it can neither be stored nor preserved. As the clock ticks, time is going, never to return. The destination is what determines if it is being lost or maximized. Every day, we are given 24 hours and as the clock ticks, the hours are diminishing till at 11pm, you have only one hour left. By 11:59 pm, your gift and treasure of 24 hours is depleted.

We should understand that life gives us a gift of 24 hours every day, which cannot be stored nor preserved so it is up to us to use or waste it. Therefore it is important to develop good time management skills. We must learn to use time and rule over time. It is important to change our attitude towards time and begin to value it.

Time cannot be bought back

Time cannot be bought back despite the price one is willing to pay. Yesterday is gone and it is gone forever. Billions of dollars cannot bring yesterday back. So no matter the amount of money you are willing to pay, once those 24 hours are gone, you cannot buy it back.

Some people lost their childhood and as adults they wish they could bring those days back. But that is simply a wish! Their millions cannot take the clock backwards. Others wish they could reset the clock and take it back to sometime in their past, but money cannot do that.

Time is the most expensive resource we have but it is given to us free of charge. Time is so costly that no amount of money can purchase it. Therefore our lost years cannot be bought back.

> *Yesterday is gone. Tomorrow has not yet come. We*
> *have only today. Let us begin.*
> MOTHER TERESA

So no matter how much you are willing to pay, yesterday is gone and gone forever. All you have is today because tomorrow isn't a promise. So in reclaiming your lost years, you should focus on today, on the 24 hours of today and maximize them.

As I said earlier, all hope is not lost. Your lost years can be reclaimed by focusing on the time you have left, the next second, minute and hour of your life.

This book contains keys and principles that will enable you to regain your lost years, achieve tremendous success, realize your goals and dreams beyond your wildest imagination. But first, you must wake up, dust off the ashes of hopelessness and stop living in regrets. It is no use crying over spilt milk. As long as you have life, you have time! And you can make the most of what you have left.

> *Anyone who is among the living has hope — even a*
> *live dog is better off than a dead lion!*
> ECCLESIASTES 9:4 NIV

There is hope for you so long as you are alive! Your lost years can be reclaimed. There are lots of people who picked up the broken pieces of their lives and turned it around.

A lot of millionaires and billionaires went bankrupt at some point in their lives but regained their wealth e.g. Henry Ford, Donald Trump etc. In fact, a lot of successful people know that to become successful, you have to fail several times. Failure is not an end; you are not a failure because you failed. You only fail when you fail to get up after a failure!

We have established the fact that your lost years cannot be recovered, so it is important to forget the past and stop living in regret. We have also explained that our focus is on today, the 24 hours of today. I want to present to you therefore, the key to reclaiming your lost years.

THE KEY TO REGAINING
YOUR LOST YEARS

It is important that in every hour of your life, you are doing either one or more of these three things:

Adding value to your life.

Adding value to others.

Producing valuable goods or services.

The key to regaining your lost years therefore, is to invest maximum value into every second, minute and hour of your day in order to produce more results. This means that every hour of your day must be filled up to its maximum capacity with so much value targeted towards adding value to you, others or producing goods or services.

By investing maximally into each hour of your day, you will be able to reclaim your lost years. Therefore, once you wake up in the morning, you must ensure that each hour of the day is loaded with maximum value to produce more goods and services than previously possible. In other words, you have to avoid minimal or mediocre efforts and results, but on purpose invest the best and highest into your hours.

What this key entails

First of all, this key means that every hour of your day must be accounted for i.e. when you look back over the last hour, you can tell specifically what you achieved. You can pinpoint the value you added in your life or the lives of others or the goods and services you produced within that hour of your life. Some people are unable to account for each hour or even the entire day. They spend a whole day without pinpointing something tangible they achieved with their 24 hours apart from sleep. This is wrong and it leads to a waste of time.

To reclaim your lost years, you must account for every hour of your day. Your time is your life therefore you ought to tell where a part of your life went to.

The key means that every hour of your day must be utilized to add value to your life or to others through production of goods and services. In other words, your time must be used to produce tangible results that are valuable either to your life or the lives of others.

It is possible to account for the past hour of your life but the products are worthless. If the past hour was not spent in an activity that adds value to your life; making you a better person, or making the life of another better or producing goods and services that will enrich the lives of people then, that hour of your life has been lost. Thus every hour should count for something that is important and valuable.

For instance, let's scrutinize the activities of four friends in the last one hour of their lives. Matthew spent the last hour watching a popular TV show, while Cynthia spent the last hour on a phone conversation, discussing the latest celebrity gossip with a friend. Ken spent the last hour researching on a project topic for his class assignment while Peter spent the last hour on the phone counseling a couple facing marital crises.

Ken and Peter added value to their lives and the lives of others whereas Matthew and Cynthia wasted a precious hour of their lives. So in reclaiming your lost years, you must ensure that your hours are filled with activities of value. In subsequent chapters, we will deal with activities that are time killers and life killers.

The key also means to invest maximum value into each hour of your life. This shows that our aim is to achieve more in every hour than we did in the past. This calls for more skill in handling our time. It entails increasing our speed and producing more valuable goods or services within the same time frame.

Reclaiming your lost years is a race against time. So it calls for maximum efficiency and speed. Because you are engaged in a fight against time, you must consciously seize every second of your day and load it with maximum value. So if you read one book in a month, how about two or three; if you baked ten cakes in a day, how about twenty; And if you wrote one book within three month; how about two? It is important to ensure maximum productivity within the allotted time in order to reclaim your lost years.

Let's consider another example using three tailors whose stores are located in a big mall. Tailor A is able to sew one dress in one hour, while Tailor B sews two but Tailor C has mastered the skills and sewing process and is able to sew 5 dresses of exceptional quality within an hour. Tailor C has added maximum value in one hour of his life by producing more goods than others.

The purpose of this book is to teach you how to invest maximum value into each hour of your day, thus regaining your lost years. In this book, you will learn how to rule over time, recover it from time killers and load it up with maximum value and maximum results.

However, the lessons in this book will demand a change of your present mindset, attitudes, habits and patterns that are responsible for your current predicament. It will necessitate a willingness to change because as they say, insanity is doing the same thing and expecting a different result. If you do not change the habits that caused you to lose your years, you will continue to lose more. So a willingness to change isn't just important, it is a prerequisite.

Secondly you ought to have a burning desire to regain your lost years. Reading this book shows that you have a desire to do so. But, an ordinary desire may not achieve the results you need. You need a burning and passionate desire to regain your lost years and fulfill your dreams and visions.

CONCLUSION

We have understood why time is our greatest earthly treasure and I believe your sense of appreciation of time has increased. Your success in life is largely dependent on how well you manage and maximize your greatest treasure called time. Therefore I urge you to commit to paying attention to every second, minute and hour of your day and ensure that you are adding maximum value to yourself, others or producing goods and services. Before you sleep at night, analyze your day and confirm that you invested maximum value into each hour. Henceforth, you will no longer trifle with time instead you will be committed to investing maximum value into each hour of your day.

In the next chapter, we will discuss another fundamental topic with respect to regaining your lost years.

THE GOLDEN NUGGETS

- Time is our greatest treasure and our

  attitude to it needs to change positively.

- Our lives are calibrated in time.

- Everything we see is a product of time.

- Your success depends mainly on

  how you manage time.

- The important matter is not the time you lost

  but how to manage the next hour of your life.

- The key to reclaiming our lost years is to invest

  maximum value into each hour of the day.

CHAPTER 3

DISCOVER YOUR
LIFE PURPOSE

We have learnt that the key to regaining your lost years is to invest maximum value into each hour of the day so as to produce maximum results. In this chapter you will learn the areas of your life where you should invest the major part of your time. You will also learn about Purpose, its meaning, significance and how to discover your God-given purpose. In addition, you will kick-start the process of reclaiming your lost years by learning how to be organized in all your daily activities.

DISCOVER YOUR PURPOSE

The first step to regaining your lost years starts with the discovery of your purpose in life. Many people have no destination in life and if you don't know where you are going then any road can lead you there. You were born for a specific assignment. You were not born to be a jack of all trades, master of none. You were not called to do many things in life, instead, you were made for a particular purpose and it is imperative to discover it and fulfill it.

Purpose is the reason for your existence. It is what you were designed to accomplish while on earth. Therefore you ought to discover what it is and channel your time and energy into fulfilling it. In case you have lost your years in the wrong path, pursuing a goal that has nothing to do with your purpose, it will be foolishness to continue in that wrong path. Instead you ought to use this opportunity to discover your purpose so that you can channel your time and efforts properly.

Finding your purpose starts with answering some soul-searching questions like *"Who am I? Why am I here? What are my strengths?"*

A young man who is a third year Medical student told me that he was in Medical school simply because of his intelligence and everyone, which includes his family, teachers and classmates expected him to read Medicine and Surgery. That was why he applied to read the course. He explained that he never sat down to find out what he really wants to be or what God designed him to be. He was simply following the expectations of the people in his life.

And I have discovered that there are a lot of people like that who have never taken the time to find out what their purpose is. They are clueless about Purpose and its importance to our lives on earth.

According to Dr. Myles Munroe, when the purpose of a thing is not known, abuse is inevitable. There is a reason why God created you. Nobody is a mistake, but you must do an inward search to discover the purpose for which God created you.

Purpose is what gives life a meaning.
C. H. PARKHURST

This statement shows that purpose is all we are living for. Our lives must be centered on our purpose for it to be meaningful. A life outside of your divine purpose is a life of emptiness and vanity. If you were created to be a musician and you lived all your life as a medical doctor, you did not fulfill your purpose. If you were created to be an entrepreneur but you lived as a teacher, you have failed to fulfill your purpose in life.

Your purpose may be found in your passions, talents, dislikes etc so the answers to these soul-searching questions may provide a clue to what your purpose is. "What are my passions?" "What do I enjoy doing and which I can do for no financial remuneration?" "What do I do so much that I fail to observe the passage of time when I am engaged in it?" "What do I do so effortlessly unlike a lot of people?" "What are my gifts and talents?" "What are my hates and dislikes?" "What abilities do others see in me?"

To learn more on how to discover your purpose, please refer to my book titled *WHO AM I?, WHY AM I HERE?*

Regaining your lost years entails fulfilling your God-given purpose. This means your focus is on the divine reason why you are here on earth and not your personal desires or pursuits. If you regain your lost years and invest it in the wrong pursuit, the main objective of regaining the years has been defeated. Therefore it is mandatory to find out our life's purpose and work to fulfill it.

BE GOAL-ORIENTED

Having discovered your purpose, it is vitally important to strategize on ways and means to achieve it. Therefore it is important to set goals that are tailored towards the achievement of your purpose. Set goals, list everything you want to achieve within the day or week or month and year, set your deadlines then begin to work towards them.

To be goal-oriented means to plan your life, career and all your activities around your purpose. Assuming your purpose is to be a baker, you need to plan your life and all your activities towards developing your baking skills. All college degrees or certification courses should be bakery-related. Most seminars or conferences you attend should be tailored towards developing and improving your competence as a baker.

Although this sounds very simple, yet many people are studying one thing whereas their dream is another. Doing anything outside of your purpose will lead to an unfulfilled life at the end.

Some people are reading courses in the University that is not connected to their purpose for several reasons. It could be to please their parents, who are trying to fulfill their own selfish desires or to live their own lives through their kids. Some parents who had unfulfilled dreams impose their dreams on their children without realizing that their lives are different from their children's. Their children have their own God-given purpose as well and it is not to fulfill their parent's dreams.

In some cases, children are forced to continue with their parent's vision especially if it is a successful one. This is the reason why some pastors raise their children to take over the pulpit when they retire whether they have a calling to be a pastor and to be in the ministry or not. Their child may be called to be a Medical doctor and to save lives through medical practice rather than through preaching. Others raise and expect their kids to take over their businesses although the child may not have any interest in running a business. Parents should help their children to discover their God-ordained purposes and refrain from imposing theirs on them. This will enable their children to live fulfilled lives.

In certain cases, some people get into the wrong professions due to popular opinions. Some professions are rated as the highest and being in those careers is a boost to the ego. Unfortunately these people's ego is boosted at the detriment of their fulfillment in life.

Whatever your purpose is, that is where your blessings are deposited. There is no career that is better than others. Purpose is what determines your land of promise. If your purpose is to be a writer, you can be a world renowned writer and achieve such astounding success that a Medical degree cannot give you. You can be more successful as a Painter than as a Lawyer if Painting is your divine calling and you work hard at it.

So the belief that success and prosperity are tied to certain professions is wrong and must be discarded. J.K Rowling, author of the popular Harry Porter series became a billionaire through her writings. Find out your purpose and focus on being the best in it. The scripture says that diligence in any work will bring you to the top. So the deciding factor is your diligence in your chosen career, and not the career itself.

Some people also are in the wrong jobs because of their financial responsibilities. They hate what they do, but have no other option. In fact, having a job is a miracle in itself. There are unemployment problems in most countries of the world and having a job is something to be thankful for. In case you found yourself in such circumstances, this is not an excuse to remain where you are. It is important to discover your purpose and begin to transition into it because that is where your success and fulfillment lie. The essence of this book is to teach you how to make your life a success in the area of your purpose despite when you switched.

Having discovered your purpose, the next step is to set your goals on how to achieve it. Without goals, your purpose is simply an illusion. It will not come to reality.

HOW TO SET SMART GOALS

Goals should be set in accordance with your purpose in life. It is important to set SMART goals. SMART is an acronym that stands for;

S — SPECIFIC

M — MEASURABLE

A — ACHIEVABLE

R — REALISTIC

T — TIMELY

Your goals must be Specific: This means that you ought to have a particular end in mind. For instance, 'I want to be rich' is a vague goal. A more specific goal would be "I want to be a Millionaire in USD in 5 years."

Your goals must be Measurable: This means that there must be metrics to judge if the goal is being attained. In this case, your bank statement and other financial documents will attest that you are making progress towards the achievement of your goal.

Your goals must be Achievable: It makes no sense to set a goal of being an Olympic gold medalist in athletics if you hate sports. You must have some interest in sports before you can set such a goal for yourself. Therefore your goals must be pleasurable and inspiring to get you on your feet.

Your goals must be Realistic: Well, if you do not have a job or a business, a goal to be a millionaire in USD in one year may be far-fetched.

> *Your goal should be just out of reach,*
> *but not out of sight.*
> DENIS WAITLEY AND REMI WITT

This means you should set goal that are challenging but achievable.

Your goals must be Timely: it is important to have a set time to achieve your goal. When do you want to be a millionaire in USD? Is it in 1 year, 2 or 5 year's time?

> *A goal is a dream with a deadline.*
> NAPOLEON HILL

Thus have a time span for your goal.

Having set your goal, you must organize yourself to ensure that every second of the day is loaded with so much value targeted towards making your goal a reality. You must become conscious of your goals and in every hour, you should be taking steps to actualize them.

BE EXTREMELY ORGANIZED

The act of being organized means to arrange in a systematic way; to be orderly, neat, tidy, methodical and efficient. It connotes having one's affairs in order so as to deal with them more efficiently. Being organized helps you to conserve time and be more productive.

Let us consider two wardrobes belonging to two friends who are also roommates. In wardrobe A, all the items are neatly arranged in individual shelves. However wardrobe B has all the items, clothes, jackets, belts, ties, mixed up in the shelves, while some are strewn all over the floor. It does not require extra intelligence to tell that getting dressed in the morning will be easier and faster for the lady who has Wardrobe A than B.

Being organized is a time saver. It increases your efficiency and enables you achieve more within any given amount of time. To regain your lost years, you must develop the habit of being extremely organized.

WHERE TO BE ORGANIZED

1. Be organized in all your daily activities.

You need to ensure that every activity is channeled towards achieving your goals. This demands that you question everything you do on a daily basis, how is this activity helpful towards the attainment of my goals?

Organize your life around your dreams and watch them come true.

UNKNOWN

This quote explains it succinctly. When you organize all your daily activities around your goals, you will achieve them.

A lot of people are involved with activities that have no correlation to their life goals. They claim they are pursuing their goals but none of their daily activities will lead them to the attainment of their goals. They are simply chasing shadows. It is important to do something daily that will bring you closer to your goals.

For instance, if your goal is to be a world class chef, then you should be studying the subject, researching about it, reading articles and magazines, learning from culinary books. It is imperative to subscribe to groups and online associations that are related to cooking; attend workshops, seminars and find opportunities to practice and sharpen your skills, take some form of formal education if necessary e.g. a college degree.

So every day, you are doing one or two things that will make you better concerning your goals. Every day, you are developing your skills, familiarizing yourself with your goal, and adding value to your life. These activities increase your belief in the realization of your goals. Your goals will not seem far-fetched and your confidence will grow, believing that one day, you will achieve your dreams.

But if your daily activities are not related to your goals, your goals will seem more difficult to achieve and more intimidating to you. The fear will make you to push your dreams farther into the future. Most times our dreams are daunting and it takes courage to pursue them. But if we would take tiny steps every day, by engaging in activities that are goal-related, it would become easier and more feasible. This is summarized by the words of Don Lancaster, an American author and inventor.

Most "impossible" goals can be met simply by breaking them down into bite size chunks, writing them down, believing them, and then going full speed ahead as if they were routine.

DON LANCASTER

Take those small steps towards your goals and make them a daily routine and before you realize it, you have achieved that huge and formidable dream. The journey of a thousand miles begins with one step, so take a step everyday towards the achievement of your goals and it will become a reality.

For instance, a person who desires to be an Olympic champion but visits the gym twice a week is not ready to compete in the Olympics yet. Others with similar dreams practice daily and compete in tournaments to keep in shape and perfect their skills. They engage personal trainers and any professional service that is needed. And it is no miracle that they emerge as champions years later. But if you are not taking daily steps towards your goal, you may never achieve it.

According to the words of Stephen Covey, *"Once you have a clear picture of your priorities, that is your values, goals, and high leverage activities, organize around them."* So in regaining your lost years, organize your daily activities with your goals as the focal point and watch them come to pass. Therefore, regaining your lost years is not about being busy doing just anything; rather it is about doing what will bring about the fulfillment of your established goals.

2. Be organized in being result-oriented

You need to organize yourself to be result-oriented. It is not about being busy rather it is about producing results. Some people are busy doing nothing because there is nothing to show for the time they spent. That is self-deception. Once you develop the habit of being result — oriented, you will have substance for the time you invest in any activity. To develop the habit of being result-oriented, it is needful to have the end in mind and then work towards it. When you know your destination, you are more likely to arrive there. Target your energy towards the attaining that end i.e. that goal.

Two students went to the library. One wanted to complete the teacher's assignment while the other went because they were mandated to vacate the hostel and he had nowhere else to go. All things being equal, the student with a goal in mind will produce result instead of the aimless one. When there is a goal in mind and you work towards it, you will achieve it. But if you did not plan to achieve anything, then nothing would be achieved.

To reclaim your lost years, do not keep busy, rather achieve results. Ensure that you have a tangible substance for the time you invested in any goal-oriented activity. If you register to attend a seminar, ensure you learn something. People can listen to a trainer without learning anything because they are not paying attention. Make it a goal to produce results every day. Be a result-driven person. Being result-oriented is about asking yourself 'what did I achieve within the past hour?' when you set your mind on achieving results that are goal-oriented, you will make faster progress towards your goals.

3. Be organized to invest maximum value into every hour

You must be organized to invest maximum value into every second and minute of your day. All your activities must be tailored towards maximizing each second and minute of your day. The key word here is maximum value. As earlier said, regaining your lost year is about investing maximum value into every second and hour of your life. So you must think about maximum value, the highest amount of value possible at all times. So you need to question yourself: "Can I do more? "Have I done my best here?" "Is this the best I could do?" Develop the habit of assessing yourself; it will keep you from being mediocre and challenge you to strive to do better and improve on your previous achievements.

I heard the story of the famous boxer and heavy weight champion Mohammed Ali. He was questioned about his exercise routine, the number of sit-ups he does. His answer surprised everyone. He responded that he didn't know because he starts counting when he is tired and ready to quit! Others count their sit-ups from the first but he starts the count when he is tired and ready to stop. No wonder he achieved tremendous success in his boxing career.

Aim towards achieving the maximum results in all your activities. That means the Olympic hopeful should aim to increase his workout time and routines and do better every day. Strive to do more, go higher, become better than the previous time. I remember the story of David Beckham, an exceptional footballer who played professional soccer in Europe. He disciplined himself to invest extra hours of personal practice after the team practice was over. Although everyone was exhausted after the general session, he disciplined himself to do more. Those extra hours made him perfect certain skills that made his football career a huge success.

Strive to do more. So if you are a marketer, do more, make an extra visit to those potential customers although you are tired and would like to call it a day. Spend extra time practicing on that musical instrument if you are an aspiring musician. As a student, practice more test questions on that subject so as to master the subject better; do more research, read other textbooks on that topic etc.

4. Be organized to not waste a second of your day

Every second of your life is vitally important and you must ensure that you do not waste it. You must fight for it and rescue it from time killers and load it up with maximum value. To regain your lost years, you must be organized to invest into each second and hour of your day. Being organized is a time conserver. It helps you get rid of time wasting activities and approach your goals in a more efficient manner thus improving your productivity.

Every second counts! They add up to minutes and hours. So every second must be harnessed and channeled into a goal-oriented activity. Do not waste the seconds of your life because they seem so small and insignificant. As we know, drops of water make up the ocean.

When every second counts towards adding value to your life and the lives of others; when it is invested in to improve and prepare you towards achieving your goals, then it is not a wasted second.

A second spent researching on the internet about your goals and dreams and a second spent on the piano, trying to master the keys and a second spent listening to a teacher are worthwhile seconds. However if you disdain the seconds of your life and refuse to develop a keen sense of appreciation for them because of their size, you will end up losing hours and years of your life.

Value every second of your life and invest maximum value into each one of them so as to reclaim your lost years.

CONCLUSION

In this chapter, you have learnt that to regain your lost years you must first of all discover your God-ordained purpose and set bite-sized goals to accomplish it. Therefore if you have not discovered your purpose, I encourage you to do that immediately. Take some time to do a soul-search and answer the questions I listed in this chapter. And for more information, get a copy of my book *"Who Am I?"*

Next write down your SMART goals on how to accomplish your Purpose. Then organize your daily schedule so that every day, you are doing something that will bring you closer to the manifestation of your goals.

In the next chapter, we will look at ways to manage time. There are certain habits that waste or kill our time. We will discuss them and it is important that you assess yourself critically to eliminate any of such habits from your life.

THE GOLDEN NUGGETS

- Identification of your God-ordained purpose is the first step towards regaining your lost years.

- Your purpose may be hidden in your passions, talents, your likes or dislikes.

- Your success is hidden in your divine purpose.

- Having discovered your purpose, you must set goals to achieve them.

- To achieve your goals, it is important to set SMART goals.

- Being highly organized will enable you regain your lost years.

- It is important to be organized in all your daily activities and make them goal-oriented.

- You must be highly organized to invest maximum value into each second and hour of your day.

CHAPTER 4

STOP DAYDREAMING

In the previous chapter, we laid the foundation to regaining our lost years which is to discover our God-ordained purpose and set goals towards its fulfillment. Now in this chapter, we will examine one habit which is a time killer but unfortunately, some of us engage in it unawares. It is subtle therefore a lot of people are not aware of the consequences of this habit. It is called daydreaming.

In addition, you will learn in this chapter how to overcome this habit and live in active consciousness.

DAYDREAMING

Some people are daydreamers. They are here but there. Although physically present and engaged in some activity, their minds are far-away, travelling from one place to another in split seconds. In other words, they are absent-minded and their minds are not fully concentrated on their current activity.

Daydreaming is defined as a short-term detachment from one's immediate surroundings, during which a person's contact with reality is blurred and partially substituted by a visionary fantasy, especially one of happy and pleasant thoughts.

Daydreamers have not learnt to control their minds so as to live in active consciousness. They may be in the classroom listening to the teacher but their minds are on mundane matters; either they are thinking about the party they attended, the new clothes they saw in the mall or what to do with their windfall etc. And they wonder why the teacher is so boring and subject very hard to understand. Some, while studying are actually thinking about their kids that are in school, the movie they watched the previous night or their upcoming party etc. Can you relate to any of these? Most people are guilty of day-dreaming to an extent. It is also true that while some workers are starring at the computer screen, they are actually thinking about their lunch, where to socialize after work or some other things not connected to their job.

Our minds are usually occupied with a lot of things and can jump from one matter to another in nanoseconds. It is a mark of indiscipline to let your mind roam. It is essential to train your mind to concentrate on the activity on hand. The mind must be trained just as the body is trained.

Living in active consciousness is about being in the here and now, and if you do not live in active consciousness, you will always be lost. You will lose time and fail to realize that your life is passing by.

CONSEQUENCES OF DAYDREAMING

Daydreaming is a great time killer

What otherwise would have taken a shorter time to accomplish will take longer due to lack of concentration.

With daydreaming, you have to invest more time to get things done than normal. But if you discipline yourself to focus on the job at hand, you will be more efficient and complete it faster. While you are daydreaming, time is flying and you are losing more years. For instance, an assignment that would have taken four hours to complete may take you six hours due to daydreaming and that means two hours are lost.

Daydreaming makes you less productive

For instance, imagine a student who spent five hours in the library studying and daydreaming. Although he spent five hours, the productive hours may actually be three hours. He had lost two hours and those hours are lost forever.

The goal in regaining our lost years, which is to invest maximum value into every second and hour, has been defeated because although studying, he lost two hours. The amount of work accomplished is not commensurate with the time invested. The same goes with employees, although a worker gets paid for eight hours of work, it is well-known that the actual amount of hours invested is less than eight hours. If employees would invest maximum value into every hour they are supposedly working, their productiveness would increase tremendously.

The habit of living in active consciousness will not only save time but it will increase your productivity. Imagine how much you will achieve if you will only discipline yourself to give 100% attention and focus to whatever task you are involved in. You will be amazed at your level of productivity because the same amount of hours will yield greater results.

Without daydreaming, you can read more books within the same amount of time. Without daydreaming, whatever you do, you will produce more results within the same time frame. In summary you will produce more without daydreaming!

Daydreaming reduces your speed

When you are working and daydreaming your speed will be reduced. But with full concentration, your speed increases and you will achieve more within a shorter time.

In regaining your lost years, it is important to realize that you cannot work at the same speed as your younger contemporaries. They have the advantage of youth and time. So this calls for a change of attitude towards your speed of performance. You need to double or triple your previous speed.

Working more than eight hours daily is not an option, it is a necessity. You need to borrow a leaf from most successful people who work 16 to 18 hours every day. In the same vein, you cannot afford the luxury of sleeping more than six hours daily. You have got to reduce your sleep hours. This is a race against time and to win, you must change your life style, habits and attitudes.

Daydreaming reduces the quality of your output

With full concentration, you will deliver not just more but better results. This is because you are paying more attention to details unlike before. While daydreaming, you may not notice errors because your brain is multi-tasking and your attention is divided. Because you are trying to regain your lost years, you need to get rid of the habit of daydreaming in order to invest maximum value into every hour of the day.

Without the distraction of daydreaming, as a student, you will have better grades and as a worker you will work better and rise faster in your career. And as a business owner, you will deliver goods and services of better quality leading to more patronage and ultimately, more profit. Your workmanship will improve and your business will grow faster.

HOW TO LIVE IN ACTIVE CONSCIOUSNESS

To live in active conscious and stop daydreaming, it is important to query yourself every two seconds to ensure that you are still focused on the task at hand.

Ask yourself, "What am I doing now?" This question is to challenge your present train of thoughts, if it is still in line with the task you are presently engaged in. You have to be conscious of every second and minute and ensure you are present in the here and now and avoid travelling in your mind. Supposing you are reading a book, and you pause to think on what you have read, it is possible to drift from that book to another thought but when you ask yourself, "what am I doing now?", it will re-route your thoughts back to the book.

In addition to querying your present thoughts, it is very important to query every activity you are engaged in to ascertain their relevance to the attainment of your goals. Your goal everyday is to invest maximum value into each hour of the day and living in active consciousness is to ask "Am I doing that?" "Did I invest the maximum value towards achieving my goals today?" "Did I live a fulfilled life today?" You ought to continue querying yourself till it becomes a habit and you start to live in active consciousness unconsciously.

100% COMMITMENT

Another habit that will enable you to regain some of your lost years is absolute, 100% commitment to whatever you are engaged in. You need to be passionate about each activity you are carrying out. Some people may not be daydreaming but they are not passionate about what they are doing. And because of that, they cannot produce maximum results. When your heart is not involved in what you do, you will never produce the best results. A lack-luster attitude towards the task at hand will produce the same results as daydreaming would. When you lack enthusiasm, spirit and passion your output will be mediocre at best.

The holy bible admonishes, *"Whatever your hand finds to do, do it with all your might"* (Ecclesiastes 9:10 NIV).

Put in your best and your heart into anything you are doing. Let the zeal for all your goal-oriented activities consume you such that people would notice. If your goal is to be a musician, everybody around you should notice, not because you told them but by your actions. It should be obvious to every person that you are set to be a successful musician someday. Passion is life, it is energy. It drives and propels you towards the object of your passion.

The story of Jesus in the holy bible shows how a person's passion can be seen by others. He was passionate about the temple of God, his father's house. At the age of twelve, he visited the temple in Jerusalem with his parents for the annual worship. However, he stayed back at the temple while his parents travelled back to their hometown thinking that he was in the company of relatives. After a days' journey, they noticed his absence and returned to Jerusalem in search for him. After three days, they found him in the temple discussing the scriptures with the Pharisees and teachers of the law. His response to their question revealed his love for the house of God.

"Every year Jesus' parents went to Jerusalem for the Festival of the Passover. When he was twelve years old, they went up to the festival, according to the custom. After the festival was over, while his parents were returning home, the boy Jesus stayed behind in Jerusalem, but they were unaware of it. Thinking he was in their company, they traveled on for a day. Then they began looking for him among their relatives and friends. When they did not find him, they went back to Jerusalem to look for him. After three days they found him in the temple courts, sitting among the teachers, listening to them and asking them questions. Everyone who heard him was amazed at his understanding and his answers. When his parents saw him, they were astonished. His mother said to him, "Son, why have you treated us like this? Your father and I have been anxiously searching for you."

"Why were you searching for me?" he asked. "Didn't you know I had to be in my Father's house?" But they did not understand what he was saying to them. Then he went down to Nazareth with them and was obedient to them. But his mother treasured all these things in her heart. And Jesus grew in wisdom and stature, and in favor with God and man. (Luke 2:41-52 NIV)

After he began his ministry, his passion for the temple was revealed again when he went into the temple at Jerusalem and found people trading in the temple. They were buying and selling in the house of God which is a breach of the purpose of the temple. His passion ignited his anger and he drove them all out, flogging them and over-turning their tables.

"When it was almost time for the Jewish Passover, Jesus went up to Jerusalem. In the temple courts he found people selling cattle, sheep and doves, and others sitting at tables exchanging money. So he made a whip out of cords, and drove all from the temple courts, both sheep and cattle; he scattered the coins of the money changers and overturned their tables. To those who sold doves he said, "Get these out of here! Stop turning my Father's house into a market!" His disciples remembered that it is written: "Zeal for your house will consume me." (John 2:13-17 NIV)

Jesus was so zealous and passionate for the house of God that everyone could see it. His actions showed his passion. This is an example of how we must burn with the passion to see our goals come to pass.

Generate huge amounts of enthusiasm towards your goals and watch yourself succeed at it.

A person can succeed at almost anything for which they have unlimited enthusiasm.
CHARLES M. SCHWAB

According to Charles Schwab, the billionaire steel magnate, unlimited enthusiasm or passion is an important key to success in achieving our goals. Enthusiasm and passion will give you the drive to pursue your goals, overcome obstacles and achieve success. Without passion, you will produce mediocre results in everything you are engaged in. but with passion, you will be more effective and efficient. Your speed will increase and you will produce more results.

Have you met a passionless teacher? It is evident from his attitude that he does not really care about his profession and his students. He may be teaching just to pay his bill but will not achieve a remarkable success in the teaching profession. A passionless footballer will not even make the team. A passionless person will find it difficult to get hired and even if he gets hired, it will not be long before he gets fired.

Georg Wilhelm Friedrich Hegel, a German Philosopher said that nothing great in the world has been accomplished without passion. This statement is absolutely true. All great inventions in the world were accomplished by people who were passionate about their pursuits.

Most of the scientists whose discoveries have enriched our lives were people of passion. It took passion to spend hours upon hours working in the laboratories till they were successful. Thomas Edison was a passionate inventor who patented so many products. But it took huge amount of passion to experiment and fail for 10,000 times before inventing the incandescent light bulb. Without passion, he would have given up, but his passion kept him going. His passion for inventions caused him to acquire over a thousand patents in his life time.

Nothing great can be achieved in any field of life without passion from being a great parent, teacher, athlete, scientist, or musician etc. Greatness is synonymous with passion. Thus in order to reclaim your lost years, you have to apply the force of passion and enthusiasm towards the achievement of your dreams and goals.

A lot of employees are not passionate about their jobs because it is not related to their purpose. They are merely working to pay their bills, no wonder the level of un-productivity among such employees. Thus it is important to discover your purpose so as to pursue your dreams with passion and enthusiasm. Passion is about being 100% committed to your goals.

Absolute commitment will increase your output and you will produce more result. It will also enable you to invest maximum value into each hour of the day. 100% commitment will increase your efficiency in all areas of your life and will enable you to regain lost years.

Nobody achieves success without absolute commitment. You will never be the best in any field if you are not totally consumed with passion for what you do and for your goals. And neither can you regain your lost years if you approach it in a lackadaisical manner. You must be passionate about adjusting your lifestyle according to the principles being taught in this book in order to regain your lost years.

Paul the apostle in the bible is an example of a man who tried to regain his lost years. He was not a disciple of Jesus Christ and missed the three years of walking with Jesus while he was on earth. He missed the teachings and one-on-one training the rest of the disciples enjoyed. In addition to that, he also spent some time persecuting the early church after Jesus had ascended to heaven. However after his conversion, he committed himself wholeheartedly to fulfilling his purpose as an apostle. He set aside his legal career and devoted his life to making up for lost years. His attitude could be seen in this verse.

> Brothers and sisters, I do not consider myself yet to have taken hold of it. But one thing I do: Forgetting what is behind and straining toward what is ahead, I press on toward the goal to win the prize for which God has called me heavenward in Christ Jesus.
> PHILIPPIANS 3:13-14 NIV

He refused to consider his past mistakes and the lost time, but he focused on his goal and fought hard to achieve it. His commitment led to more studies and research in the scriptures, more prayers, more evangelism and more missionary trips to many countries. His commitment paid off. His detailed studies and prayers led to more revelations from God that he wrote more than two-thirds of the New Testament. His numerous missionary trips led to more people converting to Christianity. Paul, a late entrant as an apostle ended up becoming more productive and greater than the others. He was able to fulfill his purpose successfully.

> I have fought the good fight, I have finished the race, I have kept the faith.
> 2TIMOTHY 4:7, NIV

Absolute commitment will help you to regain your lost years, be successful and achieve your goals and purpose.

CONCLUSION

We have seen the negative impacts of the habit of day-dreaming. Therefore it is smart to do a self-analysis to know if you possess this habit. And if you do, it is time to begin to query yourself every 2 seconds to ensure you live in active consciousness.

In addition, query the level of your passion and enthusiasm towards your set goals from time to time. Are you still passionate about regaining your lost years?

In the next chapter, we will look at another way we waste and kill our time. And more importantly learn how to put a stop to it. By so doing, we will be able to save more hours and minutes and invest them into our goals.

THE GOLDEN NUGGETS

- Many people are daydreamers i.e. they are absent-minded and so waste a lot of their time.

- Living in active consciousness will enable you achieve your goals faster than normal.

- Querying yourself every two seconds will enable you to live in active consciousness.

- Absolute, 100% commitment to any task will increase your efficiency.

- Our goals must be pursued with zeal and passion for maximum productivity.

- Nothing great was ever achieved without passion.

CHAPTER 5

LEARN TO SAY "NO"

According to Warren Buffet, the difference between successful people and really successful people is that really successful people say No to almost everything. In this chapter you will learn to say No to certain things and certain people including yourself in order to save your precious time. You will develop and unleash the power to say No because it is a powerful determinant of your ability to be successful in life.

Every day, there are lots of things that demand our attention and the truth is that most of these have nothing to do with our life goals and purposes. Yet we devote our precious time to satisfy these demands. No wonder we have lost so many years of our lives.

This time demands that we scrutinize all daily activities and identify their relevance to the achievement of our goals in life. As discussed in the previous chapter, in order to regain your lost years, you must strive to live in active consciousness. This entails that you query every activity to determine their relevance to your goals.

It takes tremendous discipline to say 'No' and stick to it. You may feel guilty or others may try to manipulate your emotions for saying No, but your purpose is more important than those feelings. It is essential to realize that 'No' is a complete sentence that requires no explanation. So practice saying No without any emotional guilt. When you master the power of 'No', you will discover that you will save a lot of time and invest more value into your life.

It is wisdom to take a hold of your time and your life. Take charge of your life and do not leave it in the hands of other people or circumstances. When you are able to determine what happens in every hour and minute of your day, you are a strong person. And when you can channel maximum value into every hour of your day and target it towards achieving your life goals, then you are a wise person.

FIGHT FOR YOUR LIFE

Time is the most valuable coin in your life. You and you alone will determine how that coin will be spent. Be careful that you do not let other people spend it for you.

CARL SANDBURG

As explained in the first Chapter, your time is your life therefore you must fight to regain control over your time and not be a slave to people and circumstances that will try to rule your life. You are a slave to whomever or whatever controls your time!

Many people are unable to say 'No' to people especially friends and loved ones. They respond to all their whims and caprices without realizing that whoever controls their time is actually in control of their lives.

The bible commands us in Ephesians 5:16 to redeem the time because the days are evil. This means we must be pro-

active about regaining our time from wasters and time killers and invest maximum value into them

While I was growing up in my village in Nigeria, I was
very poor and in order to gain acceptance, I made friends
with some boys who were of non-reputable character. I used
to play with these bad boys goofing around and engaging in
frivolous life style. I did not study my books and so performed very poorly academically. My routine after school
was to fetch firewood from the bush then spend the rest of
the evening playing with my aimless and goalless friends.

With just a year to complete high school, my older sister warned me that if I didn't wake up and study, I would
remain in the village forever. She challenged me to invest
my time in studying my books so as to be successful in life.
That discussion with my sister changed my life.

I began to separate myself from my friends and invested
it into reading my books. I used a lot of tricks and lies to get
away from them because I knew that I could not stand their
ridicule if they discovered that I wanted to study. I fought
for my time! I would go out to play with them then after a
few minutes, I would either sneak away or devise some lies
to take my leave.

I took charge of my life; I rescued my life from the hands
of my aimless friends and converted it into valuable products. As a result I excelled in my academics to the point
that I won a scholarship to pursue University education in
Russia.

SAY 'NO'

*The bad news is that time flies, the good news is
you're the pilot.*
MICHAEL ALTAHULER

You are the pilot of your time. You have the authority
to determine where it flies to. This is good news because
you can channel your time into activities that add value to
your life thereby fulfilling your God-given purpose. Unfortunately some people are not the pilots of their lives because
they have not mastered the power to say "No."

Say 'No' to the Good Things

This is because good is the enemy of the best. If you don't
say 'No' to good things, you will never get the best in life.
Whatever good that will stop you from striving for the best
must be rejected. Strive to avoid mediocrity in life by striving for the best.

I knew a young lady while I was growing up in my village. She was bright academically and wanted to be an accountant. She was also a very pretty girl. And her beauty
attracted so many suitors at that young age and they were a
lot older than she was. These men spoiled her with money
and gifts so she would accept their marriage proposals. But
she insisted that she wanted to attend the university before
getting married. However, these suitors would not take no
for an answer and pressurized her and her parents by showering them with more money and gifts. They painted pictures of a life of luxury and promised that they would train

her in the university as well. She caved in and got married to the richest of them after high school.

But things didn't turn out the way they had planned. She became pregnant and gave birth and began nursing her baby and the plan of a University education was postponed. Over the years, she had more kids and there were no more talks of getting the University degree. By the time I saw her, she was selling used clothes in the market. Her husband's business had failed and she needed to contribute to the up-keep of her family. Most of her classmates who were not as bright were graduates of the university, working and living a better quality of life than she.

And it occurred to me that she settled for a good life at the expense of a better life which would have been possible if she had pursued her dream of being an accountant. It is important to delay instant gratification and strive for the best instead of settling for the good.

Say 'No' to Family, Friends and Relatives

These loved ones can come up with demands that are not in line with your goals and aspirations. You have to learn to say 'No' to them. It is usually difficult to say 'No' to these people because we love them and always want to please them. But if you must reclaim your lost years and achieve your goals, you have to do what is right even though it may offend some people. Sometimes we are unable to say no because we are 'nice' and do not like to offend others. Being a people-pleaser shows a defect and a weakness in your character. You need to be strong and bold.

I know of students in the university, who were supposed to stay in school study and attend lectures but when their friends drove in, blasting loud music, smoking weed and sipping alcoholic drinks, they jumped into the cars and left the campus for some weekend parties in town. These students performed poorly academically because they allowed others to be pilots of their time.

We ought to realize that our time is a resource from God and He expects us to be good stewards of time. So you need to be accountable to your creator for how you managed and utilized your time. Others should not determine how you will spend your time because you are the pilot of your life. *"To whom much is given, much is required."*

Say 'No' to Pressures around You

Every day we are bombarded with urgent but unimportant matters that simply want to steal your time. Learn to differentiate important from unimportant matters and deal with them appropriately. A phone call may be urgent but unimportant whereas completing your research on a topic of interest may be important but not urgent. Prioritize on important agenda and say "No' to others.

You can lessen the pressures by learning to delegate tasks to people who can tackle them while you focus on important matters. For instance, a secretary or an assistant can take your phone calls or read your emails and revert important matters to you.

Say 'No' to TV, Social Media and Phone calls

These are the greatest time killers. Most people especially poor and unsuccessful ones devote the most part of their day to watching TV. Movies aren't just 90 minutes these days but they come as series and run into many hours.

Let's assume that you watch three hours of TV every day and only three movies every week. In one week, you would have spent over 25 hours just in front of the flat screen. Imagine what progress you could make towards your goals by investing 25 hours of maximum value into it. How much value could you add to your life by simply by cutting down on TV? Imagine how many books you could have read in 25 hours; how many cakes you could bake, how many clothes you could sew and how many client visit you could make in 25 extra hours every week!

Social media are not just a distraction, they are time killers. If you can calculate the number of minutes and hours you spend on social media, posting pictures, telling people about your personal matters, reading and posting comments on matters that do not concern you, you will be shocked!

Social networking already accounts for 28 percent of all media time spent online, and users aged between 15 and 19 spend at least three hours per day on average using platforms such as Facebook, Twitter and Instagram. Users between the ages of 20 and 29 spend about two hours on their social media account. 18 percent of social media users can't go a few hours without checking Facebook, and 28 percent of iPhone users check their Twitter feed before getting up in the morning. It is estimated that the average American spends at least a quarter of their work day browsing social media for non-work related activities.[1]

And some people engage in social media while at work and while they are supposedly studying, their concentration is reduced and their productivity reduced too. It is important to exercise extreme discipline on the use of social media. According to a CNN report on the use of social media among the youths:

On any given day, teens in the United States spend about nine hours using media for their enjoyment, according to the report by Common Sense Media, a nonprofit focused on helping children, parents and educators navigate the world of media and technology. Let's just put nine hours in context for a second. That's more time than teens typically spend sleeping, and more time than they spend with their parents and teachers. And the nine hours does not include time spent using media at school or for their homework.[2]

You must say 'No' to telephone calls too. Some people are so addicted to their cell phones that they are continuously making long calls, texting, surfing the internet and none of these activities has anything to do with their personal goals. Some are so addicted to their phone that they take it to the bathroom incase it rings! How many hours do you spend on phone calls? Are those calls adding value to your life or are they frivolous talks and gossips? To regain your lost years, you need to evaluate your phone calls.

For instance a friend might call you up to gossip about another person or to tell you stories about a party she attended. It requires discipline to ask yourself if that information will by any means add some value to your life and if not, to end the phone call as quickly as possible.

Say 'No' to anything or any activity that will distract you from your goals

Everything that is not working towards facilitating your life's purpose should not be encouraged. Therefore you need to query every activity you are engaged in to determine its value to you. Every activity you are engaged in should add value to your life and help you in the pursuit of your goals. Surround yourself with activities that are goal-oriented and are leading you automatically to fulfilling your goals.

Sometimes good things can distract you from your life's goals. You can engage in many good things to the detriment of the main purpose to which God called you. For instance, there are students in the University who become leaders in various organizations on campus, e.g. Student Union Government, Social clubs and Christian fellowships etc. They juggle these responsibilities alongside their regular academic work. But some do not handle theirs properly and pay undue attention to their extra-curricular roles to the detriment of their studies. Their performance declines and their grades drop. I advise students especially those who are pastors or leaders of campus fellowships to ensure that they are not distracted by their pastoral duties and fail their exams. They ought to excel in their studies because it is their main reason for being in the University.

Say 'No' to other's agenda

People usually have their own plans but their plans for the day should not interfere with yours. A family member may ask you to go shopping with her. But since you do not want to buy anything, why waste precious hours of your life walking up and down the mall in order to satisfy another person? Or a group of friends may call you up to hang out with them. That outing needs to be queried! Is it in line with your plans for the day? Spending time with friends is not bad at all but it must be factored into your plans. If you ought to be at the library and your friends want to hang out someplace, you must learn to say 'No'.

Say 'No' to the wrong type of friends

There are people who will attempt to lure you away from your goals and visions. Rather surround yourself with like-minded people who are goal-oriented and time-conscious.

As iron sharpens iron so one person sharpens another.
PROVERBS 27:17 NIV

Relating with people of similar minds will make you better. As it is commonly said '*birds of a feather flock together*'.

When you mingle with people who will motivate and challenge you, you will aim higher and perform better. When your friends are such that want to attend social functions and party all weekend, you will find your resistance to their pressures waning and before you realize it, you are living their lifestyle. But if you surround yourself with friends who are fighting to regain their lost years, all of you will make faster progress towards your goals.

I told you the story of my childhood in the previous chapter. After I escaped from my aimless friends back in the village and started studying my books, I began to perform well in my academics. And as my confidence grew, I began to mingle with my intelligent classmates and we became friends and reading partners. We began to motivate and challenge each other and I began to learn more from them. This association enhanced my academic performance.

Say 'No' to Churches, Pastors and excessive church programs

Some people spend hours upon hours in church–related activities, unending meetings and conferences thinking they are worshipping God. It is important to remember that attending Church meetings is not the same as worshipping God. Some pastors place undue pressure upon their members compelling them to spend many hours in church. They are mandated to attend church programs almost every day of the week. How much time is available to these people to achieve their goals or improve themselves since they spend most of their time in church? It is important to reiterate that whoever controls your time controls your life and you are a slave to him. A lot of Christians are slaves to their pastors without realizing it.

I heard the pathetic story of a surgeon who was about to operate on a patient and his pastor called and summoned him to leave everything and appear in church immediately! Despite the fact that a human being's life was in danger, the pastor insisted that he left the theatre. Thank God the doctor disobeyed him! It is expedient to know that some pastors do this simply to be in charge of the members' lives and this dominance is usually to enforce loyalty and membership.

Say 'No' to yourself

This is because you are your own worst enemy! Say 'No' to your desires that are antagonistic to your goals and visions. Discipline yourself and delay personal gratification in order to achieve your purpose in life. Put your goals before your personal desires. Practice self-discipline and delay instant gratification.

Say 'No' to the desire to sleep longer hours when you ought to be reading that book. Say 'No' to the desire to go shopping when you should be developing that skill. You need to say 'No' to the desire to procrastinate on any activity on your list because it isn't fun! Say 'No' to the desire to lazy around rather than work.

By saying 'No' to these time killers, you will be amazed at the amount of time you will save. Then you can invest maximum value in them using the principles that will be taught in the subsequent chapters.

60% PRINCIPLE

To regain your lost years, you need to ensure that 60% of your day hours are targeted towards the fulfillment of your purpose. 40% can be used for family, building /maintaining relationships, personal upkeep, church and other activities.

That means, if you sleep for six hours at night, you have a balance of eighteen hours. 60% of eighteen hours will be approximately eleven hours. So eleven hours should be invested into achieving your life's' goals and purposes while the rest will be used for any other thing.

With this principle at the back of your minds, you will be able to say 'No' to time killers and regain your lost years.

CONCLUSION

We have learnt the importance of "NO" in regaining our lost years. It is a complete sentence which we can use whenever the need arises without having to explain or justify it. We have also learnt that in addition to saying "NO" to others, it is important as well to say NO to ourselves, our passions and desires.

In your life, have you identified areas that you need to say No; either to yourself, family, friends, co-workers, TV, social media or cell phone etc? I want to challenge you to make the decision right now to say "NO" and retrieve your time from those time killers.

We have also learnt the importance of investing 60% of our active hours into our goals which is equivalent to about 10 hours daily. Ten hours targeted towards our goals daily will surely lead to its speedy fulfillment.

In the next chapter, we will look at another time killing technique which is prevalent in the churches especially the Pentecostals. We will expose the effects of these religious dogmas on our lives especially on our time.

GOLDEN NUGGETS

- To regain our lost years it is important to learn to say 'No' to time-killers.

- TV and Social media are amongst the greatest time-killers

- Saying 'No' helps us to redeem our precious time.

- We must say "No" to anything that tries to distract us from our goals.

- It is necessary to curtail too much religious activities and meetings.

- 60% of our day time should be devoted to the pursuit of our goals.

- It is important to surround ourselves with activities that will add value to our lives and facilitate the achievement of our goals.

CHAPTER 6

DOCTRINE OF WAITING ON THE LORD

Here we will be looking at certain wrong doctrines taught and practiced in churches especially among the Charismatics that negatively affect our productivity as individuals. These doctrines are propagated from the pulpit and have taken a strong hold in the minds and lives of the members yet they have no biblical backings. These religious dogmas have made Christians to be lazy, unproductive and time wasters.

"Waiting on the Lord' is a popular religious dogma that is prevalent especially among the Pentecostals. It connotes spending time praying and waiting for God to speak so that you can know his opinion, plans or agenda. It entails a more passive than active approach to hearing from God. Waiting on the Lord has come to become one of the greatest time killers especially among the Charismatics.

People use the dogma of 'waiting on the Lord' to avoid taking quick decisions but procrastinate on God's instructions. 'Oh, I will pray about it', and while they are waiting to hear from God, time, the most precious resource is flying by and along with it, golden opportunities.

Why should you pray about it when you have God living in you right now? The Spirit of God lives within you; He lives in your spirit. Your spirit and the Spirit of God are inter-twined and you can get the information you need as speedily as possible.

> *But you have an anointing from the Holy One, and*
> *all of you know the truth.*
> 1JOHN 2:20 NIV

Because you have an anointing or unction from God's Spirit, you have access to all the information you need. You know all things because the Holy Spirit lives in you. But we have problem accessing divine information because we have not learnt how to hear or discern his voice. Learn to walk with God and with his Spirit. Learn to hear him immediately and master his voice. Do this by developing a friendship with the Spirit of God and learning to walk with him every day. Fellowship with the Spirit everyday and make your prayer session a time of fellowship rather than a time of requests.

Once you learn to hear him, you will not need to pray about certain things because you can hear his voice. Hearing God's voice is not a privilege for pastors and bishops, rather it belongs to every child of God. Jesus said that all his sheep hear his voice.

> *The one who enters by the gate is the shepherd of*
> *the sheep. The gatekeeper opens the gate for him,*
> *and the sheep listen to his voice. He calls his own*
> *sheep by name and leads them out. When he has*
> *brought out all his own, he goes on ahead of them,*
> *and his sheep follow him because they know his*
> *voice. But they will never follow a stranger; in fact,*
> *they will run away from him because they do not*
> *recognize a stranger's voice.*
>
> JOHN 10:2-5 NIV

One of the greatest reasons why unbelievers are more productive and efficient than the Charismatic is because they do not need to pray before embarking on any venture. They engage their hearts and their minds. Once they have a passion for it, they forge ahead. They make their mistakes, learn from them but are still actively pursuing their dreams.

Apart from the time killing dogma of 'waiting on the Lord' the Charismatic have yet another which is called 'waiting for confirmation'. This takes place after they have heard from God. Even after God has spoken, they still want him to speak yet again and confirm what He had said. And some Christians wait for two to three confirmations before they will proceed with obeying what God told them! What a waste of time! There is no need to wait for confirmations if you have heard from God.

If you really want to reclaim your lost years and make the most of your time; if you want to invest maximum value into every hour of your day and fulfill your God-given purpose, then you have to discard those religious dogmas, traditions and beliefs! Say 'No' to 'I will pray about it', 'I am waiting on God" and 'I am waiting for confirmations' and take action.

We were told in the scriptures to wait till the Spirit is sent to us. Now that He has arrived, there is no need to wait anymore; it is time to take action.

The bible didn't say that we ought to wait for confirmations, rather it says that as many as are led by the Spirit of God, they are the sons of God (Romans 8:14 NIV). Being led depicts some type of movement. It implies that one is making a move towards or making advancement towards something. It means that you are not stationary 'waiting' for the Spirit rather on the move with the Holy Spirit guiding and directing your steps.

A LOOK AT THE EARLY DISCIPLES OF JESUS

We will take a look at the way the disciples of Jesus, the original recipient of the instruction to wait acted.

In the book of Luke 24:49, Jesus instructed the disciples to wait in Jerusalem and receive the Holy Spirit before embarking on his assignment.

I am going to send you what my Father has promised; but stay in the city until you have been clothed with power from on high.
LUKE 24:49 NIV

But prior to that he had given them a major instruction: He said to them, "Go into all the world and preach the gospel to all creation.
MARK16:15 NIV

But once they Holy Spirit arrived on the day of Pentecost, the waiting was over, it was action time! They began to run with the instruction to preach the gospel to all the nations. They were consumed with the passion for the mandate, that they paid no attention to any obstacle.

In contrast, Christians of these days will spend time to wait on God to find out where to go. He had already spoken: *"Go into all the world ..."* So what else do they need to hear? And even when God speaks again, they will start praying for confirmations! A lot of things we are praying to God for are unnecessary and a waste of precious time.

But for most Pentecostals, God has to speak multiple times before they can hear. And afterwards, he has to confirm it several times before they will take action.

> *Paul and his companions traveled throughout the region of Phrygia and Galatia, having been kept by the Holy Spirit from preaching the word in the province of Asia. When they came to the border of Mysia, they tried to enter Bithynia, but the Spirit of Jesus would not allow them to. So they passed by Mysia and went down to Troas. During the night Paul had a vision of a man of Macedonia standing and begging him, "Come over to Macedonia and help us." After Paul had seen the vision, we got ready at once to leave for Macedonia, concluding that God had called us to preach the gospel to them.*
> ACTS 16:6-10 NIV

The disciples first went to a city called Phrygia, but the Holy Spirit stopped them because that area was not ready for the gospel. They didn't stop and commence on a prayer session to find out God's will, they moved to the next town. Some Christians would feel that since God has stopped us, we need to wait on the Lord to find out his will and where to go or what next to do, but not these disciples. They were intense, and 100% committed to the instruction to go into all the world and preach the gospel.

They moved to another town Mysia, but the Spirit stopped them again. They were not deterred but they moved on to another city called Troas. And for the third time, the Spirit of God stopped them.

These disciples were determined to reach every town, city and village with the gospel. And when the Holy Spirit saw their passion and willingness to obey, he began to give them more specific instructions. He gave Paul a vision to go to a town called Macedonia.

God will not reveal certain things to you except you are on the move, obeying and acting on the little He has shown you. God usually reveals things in parts; he rarely shows the entire picture. So if you are waiting on him to get the full picture before embarking on His revealed instructions, you may never get it.

God will not show you the next step to take if you have not taken the first step in obedience and faith. But once you do, He will begin to reveal strategies, insight, understanding and revelation. You will start receiving more ideas and directions from him.

Many writers and artists will attest that they usually start off with just an idea of what to write or paint, but once they start, more ideas and inspiration will begin to flow. It never comes as a full package initially. But once they pick up their pens to write or their brushes to paint, more inspiration will start to flow. It rarely flows when they are inactive, but only when they are on the move.

Christians need to learn from that. God will only tell you more about that business venture when you start working with what he has told you already. God will open more doors for you when you have passed through the one he has opened. Stop waiting on God to open all the doors, He will not! Step out in faith and start working with what He told you.

But once you obey God and step out in faith with the instructions you have received, He will begin to order your steps and give you more understanding. Even if you make a mistake and take a wrong turn, God has a million and one ways to stop, correct and re-direct you. Since God knows your heart, that you love him and want to please and obey him, he will not allow you to fall into a ditch.

The LORD makes firm the steps of the one who delights in him.
PSALM 37:23 NIV

But he will not direct your path while you are sitting down and waiting on the Lord. He directs the paths of the people that are actively in motion, running with their goals and purposes and the visions they have already received from him.

Like I said earlier, this doctrine of waiting on the Lord is one of the greatest time killers because it makes one to be slow and unproductive. Precious time is lost as a result of this dogma. I personally believe it originated from Satan in order to keep the Christians from pursuing the plans and purposes of God intensely. I believe it is his strategy to keep the Christians paralyzed, unproductive and ineffective in life.

Do I wait on God? You might want to ask. Yes, I do. Personally I wait on God. I practice Solitude — we will discuss that later on in this book. I wait to receive an instruction on his next direction, his next plan or agenda. I wait to hear what God wants accomplished. And once I receive a word from God, a concrete direction, I take off. Once I know this is what I am supposed to do, I know it is right and I have peace in my heart concerning it, I start working on it immediately. I start by engaging in mental work; I do all the necessary research on the project, get all the knowledge available, strategize then I begin to implement immediately.

I do not wait for confirmation either. I need to hear from God only once and that is enough for me. I start running with whatever he has told me. My heart acts as the umpire, as the confirmation. Once I have peace in my heart concerning the assignment, I do not delay or procrastinate.

Once you receive a word from God and you have peace in your heart, the Spirit of God is not stopping you, go for it! Throw away that religious dogma of waiting on the Lord for confirmation and proceed with whatever God has told you. This will help you maximize your time and regain your lost years.

How to Know the Will of God

Here are four quick ways to know if your plans are God's will and not waste time 'waiting on God' or on a pastor for confirmation.

It is not against the written word of God.

It is in the interest of the kingdom of God.

It is good for people.

It is not against your conscience.

Then go for it!

YOU CAN SERVE GOD WITH YOUR TALENTS

Some people have a misconception that the purpose of God for their lives is only tied to serving in the church by being a pastor, evangelist or prophet etc. They assume that serving God is about winning souls, preaching the gospel or healing the sick. No, not at all! You can serve God by serving people with your gifts and talents.

Like I mentioned above, anything done in the interest of the people is service to God. Whatever you do to help humanity, make life better for people is service to God. So when you use your gifts and talents to improve the life of the common man, you are serving God.

I met a young Nigerian who is an inventor. This young man is a genius and he has lots of smart ideas. One of such ideas was a system to provide affordable housing and accommodation for Nigerians. Unfortunately, he told his pastor about it but he discouraged him. He was told that inventions and technological innovations are OK but the most important thing is to serve God, save people from going to hell and grow the church membership. So in a bid to do that, they took him away from his laboratory and made him a full-time pastor. So this young inventor started working in church, living an empty life. What tragedy! That is deception of the highest order!

You can serve God with your gifts and talents. Affecting the lives of humanity is service to God. Only people with the five-fold calling should work as full-time ministers. These are the pastors, teachers, evangelist, prophets and apostles. If God has not called you into any of these ministries, you have no business working in church as a full-time minister. Instead, go discover the gifts, talents and the purpose of God for your life and begin to affect lives with it. Use your purpose to bless humanity. This is the essence of our lives here on earth.

You can get more people saved and converted through your God-given purpose than through religious activities. Everything should not be about religion or religious activities. You can touch lives while you are fulfilling your purpose. And that should be your focus in life. Ask yourself: How can my purpose touch lives and impact them?

One can get more people saved by providing housing and by resolving their technological problems than by being a full time pastor. You can get more people saved through your restaurant business. Everything we do is an avenue to touch lives and make the world a better place. Our gifts and talents are tools that can enrich the lives of people.

You can minister to people and bring them to God through your paintings as an artist or through songs or books as a musician and writer respectively. Through your nursing skills, you can touch lives and get more people saved than if you were a prophet.

I heard a beautiful story about a young pastor who was passing through the worst season of his life. He had so many problems and at one point, he could not bear it anymore and decided to quit on God and on the ministry. So when he visited a mentor to call it quits, his attention was captivated by a painting on the wall. He could barely listen to the advice of his mentor but was transfixed by the painting. He eventually requested for the painting and it was given to him. He hung the painting in his house and spent time gazing at it. It spoke volumes to him and seemed to infuse him with inner strength and courage to keep going on. And eventually, he overcame all his troubles and emerged victorious. The painting was a picture of Jesus holding a man by the shoulder, as he steered his ship through a stormy sea.

That shows how a painter has been able to impact a life and change his destiny and the destiny of millions of people whose lives are connected to the ministry of that young pastor.

Imagine if Bill Gates were a born-again Christian, the impact he would make? He could touch billions of people by being an I.T guru than he could as a pastor. What if a born-again Christian invented Facebook or Apple? They could get millions of people saved through their inventions.

So go ahead and develop your gifts and talents and use them to serve the purpose of God for your life by touching lives.

PROPHETIC BLESSING

Another popular tradition which is also a time–killer among Pentecostal is the practice of getting a pastor's blessing before embarking on any project no matter how small it is. Some people want to start a business and they flock to their pastors to bless the plan before stepping out. Or they want to get a higher education, they request for prophetic blessings before enrolling into the college. They refuse to step out in faith to obey the leading of the Holy Spirit till they have received a pastor's blessings. These Christians act as though their prosperity depends on the pastors and not on God.

I would like to repeat this again. If your idea is not against the written word of God, if it is good for God and his kingdom, if it is good for man and it is not against your conscience, go for it! You do not need any prophetic blessings from any pastor.

Every child of God has been blessed. You do not need a prophet to bless the work of your hands. It is God's responsibility. And when God tells you to do something, it means it is already blessed because God blesses the work of our hands. You can proceed with it. A human being, a pastor or a prophet cannot bless your business more than God himself.

A young man came to see me recently and informed me that God gave him the idea to write a book. I said "Great, so why have you come to see me?" He replied that he had come for me to bless it because I am an anointed Man of God. I was very angry with him but I decided to advise him instead of blessing him. "How could God tell you to do something and you are coming to me to bless you? What if I dissuaded you from pursuing it, what would you do?"

God had already told him what to do but he wanted my blessings before proceeding with the instructions of the Almighty God. That is an insult on God and a waste of precious time!

Once God gives you an idea; if it is not against the written word of God, if it is good for God and his kingdom, if it is good for people and it is not against your conscience, run with it! You do not need any pastoral or prophetic blessings! Rather go to work developing the idea God gave you. Do your homework, do your research, get all the required knowledge and go for it! Stop wasting time, stop wasting life and stop ridiculing the God who gave you such ideas.

CONCLUSION

In this chapter we have seen that the religious dogmas of 'waiting on the Lord' and 'waiting for confirmation' are time killers which should be avoided. In addition the practice of seeking prophetic blessings from a pastor before embarking on any project is unnecessary. It is expedient to emulate the early disciples and be on the move, avoid procrastinations and delays.

So far, we have identified ways through which we waste or kill time and how to stop such practices. By eliminating time wasters, you have been able to regain hours and minutes of your day. In the subsequent chapters, you will learn how to invest maximum value into each hour of your day.

Recall that in Chapter 2, we said that the key to regaining your lost years is to invest maximum value into each hour of the day. In the next chapters, we are going to deal with ways to ensure that each hour of the day is loaded to full capacity with maximum value.

GOLDEN NUGGETS

- The doctrine of waiting-on-the-Lord is a great time-killer which must be rejected.

- Once you hear from God, go for it! No need for confirmations.

- It is important to familiarize ourselves with the Spirit of God in order to recognize his voice.

- God reveals more information to those who are working with what He's given to them already.

- You can serve God with your gifts, talents and calling by serving humanity and impacting lives positively.

- There is no need to seek Prophetic blessings before embarking on divine instructions.

- God's will is not against the written word of God and not against the interest of God's kingdom.

- The will of God is good for humanity.

CHAPTER 7

BE INTENSE

In this chapter, I will be bringing you about the most powerful principle that will enable you to regain your lost years. This principle is the most important word you must remember when it comes to regaining your lost years. It is the secret behind many individuals who regained their lost years. In fact it is the secret behind nations who moved from third world status to first world status.

This principle is called Intensity. Intensity refers to a state of being intense. Now let us look at the dictionary definition of the word intense as a prelude to understanding the practical meaning of it.

According to Merriam-Webster's Learner's Dictionary, intense means: Very great in degree; very strong; done with or showing great energy; enthusiasm or effort and *of a person*; very serious. Intense also means of extreme force, degree, or strength. It means to exist or occur in high or extreme degree. Other synonyms include fervent, passionate, ardent and strong.

The ability to be intense in everything is a key factor in regaining your lost years. Based on the dictionary definitions, the ability to exert extreme force or strength in every goal-oriented task will restore to you, your lost years. Secondly, it means the ability to engage very great energy, enthusiasm, and effort in the achievement of your goals will restore your lost years. Thirdly, it means that the ability to be extremely fervent, passionate and ardent in the pursuit of your God-given purpose will enable you regain your lost years.

Finally, being very serious and to the highest degree in the pursuit of your goals will restore your lost years.

The ability to be not only purposeful but intense will enable you to regain your lost years. This habit of intensity is not simply being passionate about your goals, but it connotes some form of force, strength, energy and of an extreme nature. It points to a high degree of exertion of strength in the pursuit of your goals. It alludes to an amount of enthusiasm that is far from ordinary.

A passionate writer and an intense writer are different. They are fervent about writing; they are both enthusiastic about writing, but the degree of the passion and enthusiasm is different. The passionate writer writes when all circumstances are conducive, and may have a healthy goal of writing several pages daily. But the intense writer approaches writing from a different perspective. He writes as though his life depended on it. He doesn't write when conditions are clement and conducive but he puts a pressure on himself to write. His writing goals are above board and somewhat unachievable for the passionate writer. There is an extreme application of energy and enthusiasm towards writing in his case.

This attitude of Intensity is a single quality that can restore to you your lost years. When you approach your goals with an extreme form of energy, strength and passion, you will achieve them quickly and regain your lost years.

THE ASIANS AND INTENSITY

To appreciate the quality of intensity which is a state of being intense, you need to look at the Asians. The Asians might not be endowed with much physical attributes of strength or power but they are very intense people. Intensity is a national trait and character among the Asians and they have utilized this trait very well especially among the Asian Tiger nations. This quality is responsible for making the Asians, some of the leading nations in the world.

Some of them gained their independence around the same time as some African nations but their intensity has made them to surpass those African nations in economic development, industrialization and increased quality of life etc.

The four Asian Tigers or Little Dragons are the high-tech industrialized developed countries of Taiwan, Si ngapore and South Korea along with the Hong Kong Special Administrative Region of the PRC (China) which underwent rapid industrialization, high technological development and maintained exceptionally high growth rates (in excess of 7 percent a year) between the early 1960s (mid-1950s for Hong Kong) and 1990s. By the 21st century, all four had developed into advanced and high-income economies, specializing in areas of competitive advantage. For example, Hong Kong and Singapore have become world-leading international financial centers, whereas South Korea and Taiwan are world leaders in manufacturing information technology. Their economic success stories have served as role models for many developing countries.[1]

These countries do not have a lot of raw materials or natural resources yet they have managed in a space of fifty years to grow their economy from third world countries to first world nations. The Asians are very intense in whatever they do. They have that special quality and they maximize it. In everything they do, they do it with the utmost intensity. In other words, they apply extreme amounts of energy, enthusiasm and effort towards achieving all their goals.

Because they are intense, they did not merely approach their economic and national development goals casually but with utmost passion and strength, working harder and faster than most countries, thereby accomplishing great feats within a shorter time. They are hard workers but in an intense manner. Their intensity is responsible for their increased productivity, increased speed, and increased value and net worth unlike other nations. Their intensity also makes them to excel in whatever they do.

In a similar manner, for you to regain your lost years, financially, academically, or in the pursuit of your God-ordained purpose, it is important to do so like the Asian Tiger countries did, by applying the quality of intensity.

The Asians are intense in every area of their lives. In academics, they excel. In fact the Asian-Americans are at the top in American schools and even in the entire society.

It's no secret that Asian-Americans are disproportionately stars in American schools, and even in American society as a whole. Census data show that Americans of Asian heritage earn more than other groups, including whites. Asian-Americans also have higher educational attainment than any other group.

They have higher educational qualifications and earn more than the whites, blacks or other groups in the US. The Asians are more educated than the whites and are found in highly professional disciplines like medicine, research, I.T specialties etc. And one of the keys behind their success is their hard work.

In the United States for instance, the Asian-American children excel in their academics, and are usually the smartest in their classes. According to researches done it has been established that Asian-Americans are not more intelligent than other kids but are more hardworking. The Asians have a tendency to believe that A's are for hard-workers while the Americans believe A's are for the smart kids. Asian-American kids are allowed no excuse for getting B's — or even an A-. The joke is that an A- is an "Asian F." They are tenacious even in hard work and that gives them an edge over other hard-workers.

CHARACTERISTICS OF INTENSITY

A character trait that is connected to intensity is Persistence. This is defined as the firm or obstinate continuance in a course of action in spite of difficulty or opposition. According to Merriam-Webster's Learner's Dictionary, Persistence is the quality that allows someone to continue doing something or trying to do something even though it is difficult or opposed by other people.

Intense people are persistent in whatever they do. They do not pursue their goals with a half-hearted attitude but with a die-hard quality of persistence. They are obstinate about achieving their goals. They do not give up or give in to challenging situations and circumstances. They are determined to achieve their set out goals and objectives.

When you are intense about regaining your lost years academically, the challenges of numerous assignments, projects and increased course load coupled with your job will not deter you. For example, if you enrolled in college so as to get that degree you have always wanted and you are combining your college work, projects, assignment and research with your present nine to five job, you will face a lot of daunting circumstances. But with persistence you will sooner or later receive your certificate.

Speed

Speed or rapidity is a special quality associated with intensity. Intensity connotes the attribute of working with speed. When you are intense, you invest maximum energy and you deliver results speedily. Whereas tenacious people are persistent, they are not necessary fast. Tenacity is being able to do things for a long time and persist at it but when one is intense, you do things for long but you do it with speed. Intense people combine persistence with speed or rapidity while tenacious individuals are simply persistent at whatever they are doing.

Intensity vs tenacity

Tenacity is a wonderful attribute because it combines a die-hard, obstinate quality to see your goals achieved but it lacks the quality of speed. But intensity combines tenacity with the consistency of speed. Speed is an important part of being intense. The Asians grew their economy from third worlds to a first in a very short time.

Just like Intensity is an integral part of the character traits of the Asians, tenacity is a national trait for Nigerians. Nigerians are very tenacious people. They are persistent in whatever they do. Their doggedness and determination is responsible for their success. Despite harsh conditions, Nigerians always persist to create something good for themselves. Despite the harsh economic climate and the poor leadership in their country, the average Nigerian is bent on surviving and will persist in pursuing his goals. However Nigerians also love pleasure. Although they are tenacious in pursuing their goals they may be distracted by pleasure or other secondary matters right in the middle of their pursuit.

But an intense person is so consumed that he does not notice any distractions at all. He does not see any pleasure but is focused and totally consumed with what he is doing till he achieves his goal.

For example, if a Nigerian and a Chinese were given financial loans to start a business. And both set out to do so. But in the course of establishing their businesses, both men lose their fathers. The Nigerian, because of his love for pleasure may take a part of the loan and organize a befitting burial for his father. He would throw parties in the process and satisfy all the cultural demands. But the Chinese may not touch his loan but will bury his father without incurring much expense. The love for pleasure has distracted the Nigerian from his goal of building a mega business with his loan.

Tenacity is a good trait to possess but when you have intensity, you will produce more results within a shorter period of time. However, because you are in a race to regain your lost years, the attribute of tenacity will not suffice. Rather the quality of intensity is imperative so that you can work with speed and produce more results within a shorter time.

You could be tenacious and remain so for a long time because you are being patient. Intensity does not have that attribute of waiting for a long time; rather it is result-oriented. In regaining your lost years, you do not have enough time to wait for results, younger people can afford to be tenacious but when you have lost some years, it is important to build on the character of intensity. To maximize your remaining years, you need to put intensity to work.

To develop the habit of being intense, study the Asians and learn from them. It is the hallmark of their personality. They have made intensity to work for them economically, intellectually and in all areas. To regain your lost time, study and imitate them.

Singapore grew their economy from a third world to a first world nation in a very short time. And today the cost of living in Singapore is much higher than many nations including the US. Currently it has the highest cost of living in the world.

"SINGAPORE — The Republic has emerged as the world's most expensive city to live in for the third consecutive year, narrowly edging past its rivals even though consumer prices have been slipping, a report by the Economist Intelligence Unit (EIU) showed".[2]

When it comes to education, they are one of the most competitive in the world. Times Higher Education placed National University of Singapore (NUS) at number 26 among the top 100 universities in the world and number 1 in Asia.[3] Financial Times ranked National University of Singapore's Executive MBA 11th globally in 2009.[4] Singapore has been ranked as Asia's top City of Opportunity and third amongst 30 cities worldwide by PricewaterhouseCoopers.[5]

Intensity helps you to shorten the time of execution. For example, Singapore gained independence at the same time as most of the African countries but because of their intensity, to produce maximum results within the shortest possible time, they were able to grow their economy so quick and became a first world nation.

South Korea did same too. Fifty or more years ago, they were a very poor and undeveloped country. But using the quality of intensity, they grew and transformed their country from third world to first world.

South Korea has the fourth largest economy in Asia and the 11th largest in the world. South Korea is famous for its spectacular rise from one of the poorest countries in the world to a developed, high-income country in just one generation. Per capita GNP in South Korea rose from US $87 in 1962 to US $3,145 in 1988 and to US $10,543 in 1996. The Koreans transformed their economy from an impoverished, agrarian, developing state ravaged by the Korean War to the ranks of elite countries in the OECD and the G-20. South Korea still remains one of the fastest growing developed countries in the world following the Great Recession. It is included in the group of Next Eleven countries that will dominate the global economy in the middle of the 21st century with GDP of 1,4 Trillion dollars.[6,7]

So if nations could apply the principle of intensity to regain lost years and achieve significant results within short periods of time, then you too can.

Result-oriented

Intense people are result-oriented. They combine speed with extreme forms of energy and enthusiasm in order to achieve one thing — results. They are not satisfied with being busy and being diligent. They concentrate on producing results. All their energy is geared towards result.

Intense people are not easily distracted from their goals. They are totally committed and focused on achieving the best possible results. They do not combine work with pleasure; they are very serious about the task they are engaged in.

People of Intensity are not just result-oriented, but they produce more results within a shorter time. Because they approach every task with a high degree of effort and energy, they produce more results than a person who inputs normal effort. Better and higher quality of results can be achieved by being intense.

Pressure-driven

Intense people put a lot of pressure on themselves to achieve their goals. They have an inner drive, a strong motivation to achieve their goals. Many people cannot be intense, because intensity demands putting pressure on yourself to pursue your goals. And this pressure is usually internal not external. This inner pressure drives an intense person to go farther and do much more than the ordinary person would undertake.

An intense person is driven by an internal pressure to achieve his goals. Most people are driven by an external pressure to pursue their goals and when the pressure is gone, they return to the status quo. For instance, most students study hard when the examinations are close. They begin to study for hours, burn the midnight candle and cut down on all their usual activities. They conduct research, revise what they were taught and study their textbooks because of the forthcoming examinations, an external pressure. And after the examinations, they would resort to the lifestyle of complacency and pleasure till another examination wakes them up again. They are stimulated by external pressures. And once it wears off, their efforts wane.

But an intense student studies everyday as if he were preparing for an examination. He has an internal pressure to excel in his studies and it puts on him the same amount of pressure as an approaching examination would. He reads beyond his class curriculum, he reads wide. He researches deeply and extensively and is ready for any impromptu test or quiz. His involvement in extra-curricular activities is low because his goal is to excel academically.

That is the attitude that you must imbibe to regain your lost years in any area of your life.

EXAMPLES OF INTENSE INDIVIDUALS

Recently I started an online coaching program where I teach my mentees life changing sermons. I preached for one hour every morning and every evening, seven days a week. After four months of these super-intensive training, my mentees began to complain that they were unable to keep up with the rate at which they were receiving such wonderful teachings. They wanted to know how to apply the principles and still maintain the pace with me. Others wondered how I could maintain the tempo and teach them twice everyday despite my busy and heavy workload.

I laughed as I told them that it was their responsibility to solve their dilemma. But as for me, I was practicing and sharpening my intensity skills. Personally, I discovered that trait in me and over the years, I took time to sharpen it. It took four hours for me to prepare my training topics and two hours to deliver it to them. Yet for six months I have consistently delivered it to my mentees twice every day.

I had a reason to practice intensity because I am also competing against time. Although I have been a pastor for many years and have done a lot of exploits, I have been unknown to the rest of the world. Rather I was hidden behind the iron curtain of Russia and Ukraine and was practically unknown even to my fellow Nigerians. So when God asked me to return to my country and transform it, I knew it was time to come out of hiding. It was time to showcase myself to the rest of the world and raise disciples.

My international publicity was poor, so to regain my lost years in that area, I had to put intensity to work. And unlike other pastors who do online coaching programs once or twice weekly or when it is conducive for them, I had to double and triple mine. And so consistently for over 6 months, twice a day, and seven days a week, I have been working, training, coaching and mentoring and changing the lives of my followers. My followership is increasing and lives are being changed.

Intensity will double or triple your speed and restore your lost years back to you. If your goal is to rebuild your financial portfolio, you can apply the principle of Intensity to double your speed. This means that you will approach the process of savings and investments with an extreme amount of enthusiasm and energy unlike an average person. Your measures may be seen as very drastic by others but it will yield results in a shorter time.

Thus, instead of saving the usual 10% of your income that many advocate, you will need to save more. I usually recommend saving 30% of your income for people who are not racing against time, but the more you can save the better. Secondly saving will not be done when it is convenient; rather you must save religiously on every pay check. Intensity will also be demonstrated in the way you cut off your frivolous lifestyle and live within your barest minimum. And finally, it will be seen in your efforts to grow your money. But practicing intensity will get you to your destination faster than others.

That was how I became a millionaire. I had grown my church to be a millionaire church by practicing some laws of money that I had learnt. Prior to that, my church had a monthly income of 40,000 USD, but before the end of the month, we were in the red. The income was simply not enough to meet all our needs and cover our expenses. But when I discovered the laws of money and practiced it on the church finances, it became a millionaire church within two years! From a monthly income of $40,000 to a Millionaire status in two years!

So I decided to practice these same money principles on my finances too. I gave myself a target of two years, but I became a millionaire in US Dollars in 9 months! That's the power of intensity. It can restore to you, your lost years!

I have told the story of my childhood, growing up as a poor boy in my village in Nigeria. I was very backward academically that my teachers used to give me hard knocks on my head because they were amazed at my level of dullness. They said that no one from my family was dull; rather they were quite smart academically except me.

I thought intelligent people were created like that and didn't know anything about reading or studying one's books in order to perform well academically. I didn't realize that my classmates who were bright studied their books. I never read my books. I lived with my grandmother in the village and whenever I returned from fetching firewood in the bush, I spent the rest of the evening playing with my friends. Until my sister visited and advised me to start studying my books in order to perform well.

I had just one year left to take my final high school examinations. I was fighting against time. I needed to cover a five-year syllables in one year. Although I didn't realize it then; but I engaged the principle of intensity. I converted my play hours into study time and began to invest six hours every day into my studies. Once I returned from the bush with the firewood, and escaped from my friends, I would face my studies. I took it subject by subject and devoted six hours studying them. For instance, when I pick up mathematics, I would study it for six hours. Then the next day, I would pick another subject, say English language and invest six hours into it. Before I realized it, I found that those subjects were not so difficult and complicated after all. Mathematics was simply formulas, I realized.

My intensity paid off handsomely and I performed so well in my exams that I won a scholarship to pursue a university program in Russia. In one year, through the power of intensity, I moved from being the worst student in my class to one of the best! Make intensity a habit and watch it deliver to you, your lost years! This single quality is a major key to regaining your lost years.

I heard the story of a multi-millionaire who is an expert in the multi-level marketing business. Before he made his millions, he called his family together and told that of his plans to become a millionaire and achieve financial independence. Then he requested for one year off from his duties as a dad and a husband. They may not see him every day, he will not come for their school plays and games and will not be present at dinners etc but at the end of one year, they could ask for anything they wanted and he will give it to them.

That is intensity! So he set out on his mission to become financially independent in one year. However because he engaged the force of intensity and took steps that were 'abnormal' he achieved his goal within 9 months instead. And he kept his promise to his family too, and bought them everything they wanted!

CONCLUSION

We have learnt why intensity is the most important word you should remember when it comes to regaining your lost years. We have seen the principle in practice in people's lives as well as in nations particularly, the Asians.

We have seen that tenacity is not enough to reclaim your lost years because it lacks the quality of speed. Therefore it is important to cultivate the habit of being intense. Any habit can be cultivated. The chain smoker was not born that way. He cultivated the habit of smoking by constant practice.

Therefore, I challenge you to make cultivating the habit of Intensity your number one priority. Once you develop this singular habit, you will not only reclaim your lost years but you will discover that your level of productivity has soared.

In the next chapter, we will discuss another principle that will enable you to invest maximum value into each hour of your day.

THE GOLDEN NUGGETS

- Intensity is a single key through which you can regain your lost years.

- The Asians are very intense people and intensity is the key to their success.

- The success of Asians in Diaspora is attributed to their intense nature.

- The success of the Asian Tiger nations can be attributed to their intensity.

- Intensity enables you to double or triple your speed.

- Intense individuals exhibit a strong degree of energy and enthusiasm towards the achievement of their goals.

- While Nigerians are tenacious but lack speed, Asians are intense and have speed.

- Intense people are pressure-driven, result-oriented and fast.

- The single habit of being intense in the pursuit of any goal will surely make you a success.

.

CHAPTER 8

THE POWER OF FOCUS

As we all know by now, the key to regaining our lost years is to invest maximum value into each hour of the day. And in this chapter we will discuss another principle that will help us achieve that. It is called the power of Focus.

Focus, according to the dictionary means to fix (as one's attention) steadily toward a central objective. It means to fasten, center, rivet or concentrate on something. Focus means to pay particular attention to or concentrate on something. When you focus on a thing, you direct all energy towards the object of your attention and it enables you to achieve more result than otherwise. There is power therefore in focus and concentration.

But I would like to describe the power of focus using the laser technology. Let's consider the electric bulb hanging in the room where you may be sitting right now. It provides light to brighten the entire room. It provides a little bit of heat but not enough to burn your skin or the items in your room. It is not powerful enough to heat your water or cook your food. This is because the light energy from that bulb is dissipated. It has some amount of energy or power but because it is dispersed, you cannot use it except to brighten a room.

However, when the principle of laser is introduced, the same light rays will be totally different. The laser technology employs a laser which is a device that concentrates the light rays many times over till it emerges as a single but powerful beam capable of so many things.

This single laser beam is so powerful that it can penetrate through materials that ordinary light cannot. It can cut through clothing materials, skin and through metals. Laser beam can produce a lot of heat to cook your food, burn your skin or burn the whole house down. By focusing and concentrating those otherwise weak and dissipated light rays, a single but powerful beam was produced. That is the power of focus!

When you focus and concentrate your energy and attention into any given task, you will achieve huge results. In regaining your lost years the ability to focus and concentrate on the task at hand like a laser beam will help you invest maximum value into that hour. Assuming you were given one hour to accomplish a task, the amount of value you are able to produce within that hour depends largely on the power of your focus and concentration.

Angela and Christy are both colleagues and friends. They work in an insurance company. They are both married and have little children. Recently they attended a financial seminar and learnt about having more streams of income. Since both share a passion for baking cakes they decided to supply cakes to a supermarket in order to make more money. They did the market survey and found shops willing to accept their goods. Due to their jobs and their families, they have only weekends to engage in their part-time business.

Angela decided to give this business her full concentration. She did a lot of research during her free time on how to bake good quality cakes and different types of cakes. She studied the different flavors and their market demand. She invested some of her savings to purchase some equipment that will make her work faster as well as every other utensil she needed. Then she re-organized her kitchen and created a special corner for her bakery. She labeled all the cabinets and arranged the ingredients for easy access. Then she created her recipes and arranged them neatly in a file.

Then came Saturday, before her kids and her husband were up, Angela was in her special bakery corner mixing her cakes. She didn't turn on the TV for the early morning shows, but she focused on her baking. By noon, she had fifteen dozens of cupcakes cooling on her kitchen cabinet ready for supply.

Christy on the other hand purchased some ingredients and some utensils. She asked her daughter to put them away, but didn't know the exact cabinets where she placed them. She didn't plan on the exact type of cake to bake but would decide later. Saturday morning, she woke up at the same time as her family members and decided to prepare breakfast. After breakfast, she turned her kitchen upside down searching for some items her daughter put away for her.

Eventually she started mixing the cake but realized that she needed an ingredient, so she dashed off to the nearby store to buy it. Her husband had turned on the TV so as to enjoy the early morning shows and she watched while she baked. By noon, she had two dozens of cupcakes ready for supply as well.

What is the difference between these two friends? The power of Focus and Concentration! Angela was focused on making her new business a success and her focus and concentration made her to take steps in organizing her baking routine, getting all her ingredients ready, getting up early and turning off the TV. Her Focus and Concentration on the baking produced more cakes and earned her more money than Christy.

Christy on the other hand was distracted. Her attention was split between watching TV, conversing with her family members and baking etc. For her to excel in her new business and make more money she needs turn off all distractions and engage the power of Focus and Concentration.

With Focus, you can produce more results within a specified time than a person without focus. When you give any task your full concentration, you will produce more results within a shorter time. Through the power of focus, you can invest maximum value into every hour of your day. Through the power of focus, we can concentrate our energy, attention and skills like a laser beam and generate maximum and inconceivable results.

With Focus and Concentration, you can read an entire book in one day unlike a person who is not focused. With Focus and Concentration, you can attend to more customers on your job, produce more goods and services, maximize time and produce more value either to you or to others.

With Focus and Concentration, you will produce goods of higher quality. For example an accountant who is focused on her job, not distracted by phone calls, noisy colleagues

THE POWER OF FOCUS

or social media notifications will have fewer errors in her work. The quality of your output is enhanced by the degree of your focus and concentration.

FOCUS IN OUR GOALS

There is a proverb that says, if you chase two rabbits, both will escape. This sums up the importance of applying Focus and Concentration in all you do. When you disperse your energy into many things, you will not perform optimally in any of them. To reclaim our lost years it is important to concentrate your attention and resources into one goal at a time and produce maximum results in it.

The story was told about George Washington Carver, the African-American Botanist who improved the lives of US farmers. He was deeply fascinated by nature so he asked God to teach him about nature. But God told him that the study of nature was too vast and too big for him to understand, instead he should ask for something smaller. He asked to be taught about plants, and the response was the same, too huge. So he asked God to teach him about the peanut.

George Washington Carver devoted the major part of his career in studying peanut. He spent hours and days in the laboratory researching on peanut alone. And it is no surprise that he discovered over 300 products from peanuts! These include: cooking oil, axle grease and printer's ink, dyes etc. That's the power of Focus and Concentration! His work on peanut earned him the nickname, "The Peanut Man."

Jack of all trades, master of none!

A lot of people approach their life goals without focus. Their attention is usually taken up by too many things. Others try to do so many things at once and this spreads their energy thinly across board. Because none of their goals is getting maximum focus and concentration, they end up producing mediocre results in all of them. That is why they are Jack of all trades but not able to master any of them.

In order to reclaim your lost years, it is important to identify your most important goal and focus on achieving it. That means all of your activities must be targeted towards fulfilling that goal. However, if you try to achieve several goals at the same time, you will not be able to apply the same amount of focus on each. When you dissipate your attention into many needs, you will not achieve maximum results in all of them. When you have a lot of activities competing for your time, you will only give average value to each of them. So the principle of focus is very important in achieving maximum results in any objective or goal we have.

The power of focus will make you a master in any endeavor or goal you've established for yourself. For instance, if your life purpose is to be a chef, you have to focus all your attention on it. But if you divide that attention to pursue a career in music, your focus will be divided and you will not give both a 100% commitment.

If you concentrate on developing your culinary skills, you can sharpen your skills, create excellent recipes, start your own restaurant and build a thriving business for yourself. But when you dissipate yourself into many ventures, you'll lose the laser effect. You may decide to branch off into music when your business is fully established and be a master in music as well.

Winston Churchill said *"You will never reach your destination if you stop and throw stones at every dog that barks."*

This sums up what we have said. You cannot reclaim your lost time if you do not approach your goals with utmost concentration and avoid all manner of distractions. It is important to run with your goals and not get distracted by what others are doing. Others who have the advantage of time may diversify into many ventures all at once, but you cannot afford to join their boat. You have got to know what your purpose is and define it so well that there are no ambiguities. Then single-mindedly run towards it.

Channel all resources into developing your talents and sharpening them to make them marketable and profitable to you. Channel all resources towards acquiring the necessary skill-set that will enable you to achieve your dreams. Channel 60% of your day hours into working on your goals and avoid all manner of distraction by saying "No' to them. Think and talk of your goals at all times. Think of ways to improve, ways to work faster and accomplish your goals in shorter time. That's focus and you will achieve that goal faster than you thought possible.

CONCLUSION

We have learnt how the principle of Focus and Concentration can help us redeem our lost years. Because the effects of Focus on any task can be likened to the effects of a laser beam, you can accomplish your set goals faster. Therefore it is important to engage this principle while working, studying, researching etc. If you are a student, you will discover that you will complete your assignments faster than others. And as an employee, you will be able to meet deadlines and exceed expectations.

To practice this principle, it is important to check your habits and identify sources of distractions. It could be phone calls, social media or noisy environment or day-dreaming etc having identified these sources of distraction, put in measures to remove or minimize them. For instance, if you lack concentration because of a noisy environment, look for a quiet place. As a student, I would leave the hostels when I needed to study because it was too noisy. Instead, I went to the library.

If your cell phone notifications are the source of your distractions, then turn them off and mute your phone when you are working or studying. And if your lack of focus is due to day-dreaming, then begin to practice staying in active consciousness. You may need to refer to Chapter 3 to refresh your mind on how to do that.

I urge you to begin to unleash the power of focus in any assignment or project you are involved in starting right now. Do not allow distractions both physically and mentally and you will be amazed at your speed and maximal accomplishments.

In the next chapter, we will discuss another principle that will enable you to invest maximum value into each hour of your day.

THE GOLDEN NUGGETS

- The power of Focus and Concentration will produce results similar to the laser beam.

- To reclaim your lost years, it is important to focus on every task at hand.

- The power of Focus and Concentration will enable you to produce maximum results within a shorter time thereby restoring your lost years to you.

- The power of Focus will make you a master in any field of endeavor.

- Focus and Concentration increases your speed and improves your efficiency.

- Focus and Concentration eliminates distractions and improves the quality of your products.

- Focus and Concentration on one goal at a time increases your efficiency.

CHAPTER 9

....

ENGAGE SPEED

In this chapter, we will discuss another principle for regaining lost years. This principle does not merely deal with investing maximum value into every hour of the day; instead it also shows how to do it faster than normal. We are in a race against time therefore it is important to compete faster. This principle will show you how to work faster and achieve more results within the same time frame than before.

This principle is called Speed.

The role of speed in reclaiming your lost years cannot be over-emphasized. Like earlier said, we are in a race against time therefore, it is important to run with speed.

We have said over and over that the key to reclaiming our lost years is by investing maximum value into each second and hour of the day. Speed is necessary to invest more value within the hour. We can produce more goods and services within an hour when we operate with speed. You can get more work done with speed thereby increasing our efficiency.

WHAT IS SPEED?

According to my personal definition, Speed is the ability to take a decision in less than 5 seconds. Taking quick decisions is the hallmark of successful people. Sometimes a quick decision is the difference between success and failure or life and death. Many times we drool over decisions and miss opportunities. We procrastinate on what we need to do while our precious time is flying by. In order to regain your lost years, you must be able to take quick decisions. You need to be able to harness opportunities quickly.

Our days are filled with lots of instances to make decisions. In fact, we are faced with hundreds of decisions every day. The ability to navigate through these decisions as quickly as possible is an important factor to maximizing our time. Some decisions are minor while some are major and more impactful. From the color of tie to wear, the breakfast to eat, the route to drive to work to accepting or declining the business or marriage proposal, our decisions vary in significance. The ability to take quick decisions is necessary to avoid delays.

It is needful to emphasize that we are not advocating taking blind decisions within 5 seconds or taking decision based on partial or incomplete knowledge of the situation. Rather it is about taking informed decisions quickly. Speed is about having seen both sides of the coin; you are able to pick one within 5 seconds. Therefore you must know all there is to the situation and quickly decide on a course of action. This applies to major decisions that have far-reaching consequences.

But there are more minor decisions that can kill our time if we do not handle them quickly and move on. When you train yourself to take decisions especially minor decisions very quickly, you will save a lot of time. For instance, some people take a lot of time to groom because of indecision on what to wear. This minor decision can affect your speed negatively. Women are especially prone to this habit although some men are. While they stand in front of their wardrobes trying to decide, the time is ticking. And although it may seem insignificant at first, it adds up to quite a significant amount of time. Speed is the ability to decide on what to wear within 5 seconds.

President Barack Obama says that he wears only blue or gray suits to lessen the stress of having to decide among many options and focus on important matters. Steve Jobs wore a black turtleneck to work every day while Mark Zuckerberg remains a hoodies and jeans guy. They have stated that their monotonous style is to avoid making daily decisions on what to wear. These men understood the importance of time and speed and would not waste it on minor matters.

When faced with a lot of options, people find it difficult to make quick decisions but the ability to quickly sift through these options and chose one within 5 seconds will greatly improve your time management skills.

Another minor decision like what to eat can be time-consuming for some people. These people cannot make up their minds while at the restaurant. They stare at the menu for a long time unable to make a choice and keep the waiter waiting. Instead of a 40 minutes dinner, the time is stretched to 60 minutes.

In order to redeem our lost years, we must learn to take quick decisions. A quick decision taker saves time and works with speed. But a slow decision-maker is a time-killer. And in order to reclaim our lost years, we must save and not kill time.

Sometimes as a student, there are lots of assignments to do and lots of topics to study and notes to read that they are overwhelming and confusing too. Inability to decide quickly will lead to more minutes of study time being wasted. While a slow student is taking ages to decide on the subject to study, another quick student has picked up his books and is headed to the classroom.

Taking decisions quickly can also impact your productivity on the job. Ability to decide within 5 seconds whether it is a Yes or No will prevent loss of productive hours. Quick decision takers get ahead faster than others. They are fast to decide and execute assignments and get more work done than the slow person. They are good time managers.

When it comes to major decisions, it is vitally important to do our research and get as much information as we can get and then take a quick decision. Some people, although they have all the information still hesitate on taking a decision and would prefer to procrastinate and put if off on the pretext of 'I will think about it'. This is just a time-wasting gimmick, since there is nothing to deliberate on anymore. In order to reclaim your lost years, you have to take quick decisions.

SPEED-BREAKERS

'Waiting-on-the-Lord'

In religious circles, 'Waiting-on-the-Lord' dogma is akin to 'I-will-think-about-it' syndrome. Both are strategies to procrastinate and kill precious time. As discussed in Chapter 5, the practice of waiting on the Lord and waiting for confirmations are habits that steal time. It is needful to run with any instruction God gives us and avoid wasting time praying for confirmations. Some Pentecostals after hearing from God on a course of action revert back to prayers to get a confirmation. And some resort to their pastors to confirm what God has said. These are all unnecessary. It is important to develop a relationship with God so as to hear him clearly and once you do, then run with it.

The Spirit of God lives within us and we are entitled to hear his voice as the children of God. So we are not in the dark as to what to do. All it requires is a familiarity with God so as to recognize his voice. God can speak through any avenue; through the voices of people, nature, circumstances, the Bible etc, therefore it is vital to learn to discern his voice. Whatever God tells you; if it is not against the written word of God, if it is good for God and his Kingdom, if it is good for people and it is not against your conscience, then run with it.

Mental laziness

Some people are slow to take decisions because they are mentally lazy. They have not trained their minds to think fast and then to act fast. According to Susan Wojcicki, CEO of You tube;

Work smart. Get things done.
No nonsense. Move fast.

In today's fast-paced world, you need to think fast and move fast. Do not take ages trying to get your acts together. It is imperative to move fast and that involves taking quick and smart decisions.

The Facebook guru, Mark Zuckerberg, says it with a twist of humor; *"Move fast and break things. Unless you are breaking stuff, you are not moving fast enough"*

This statement means you need to be fast in whatever you do. Take quick decisions, take risks. Don't wait till you have everything figured out before taking a decision. Some, in an effort to be cautious hesitate to make quick decisions. They fail to realize that they are killing time. Develop your minds in such a way that you will know what to do immediately. Train yourself to be able to quickly sift between available options and decide on one. When you train your mind to work quickly, sooner or later, it will be easier to make most decisions quickly.

Train yourself to take 5 seconds decision on mundane and minor matters like what to eat for breakfast, what meal to choose on the restaurant menu, where to eat lunch, how to style your hair, the book to read etc. from minor matters you can progress to important ones. As you get better at making decisions faster, major decisions will not be herculean tasks anymore.

Procrastination

To procrastinate according to the dictionary means to delay or postpone action; put off doing something.

Some people procrastinate on taking decisions. They would rather put it off till a later date in the future. But no matter how long it is pushed under the rug, a time comes when an action must be taken. And some times the cost may become higher than before. A decision to eat right and lose weight may seem trivial but when other health risks manifest, the cost of indecisiveness will become apparent. You may be overweight. You know it's unhealthy, and you know you need to get rid of the excess weight quickly. But you procrastinate and before you realize it, you wind up in the hospital sick, broken and hooked up to all kinds of machines. Your organs are failing and you have got months to live. Procrastination does not seem cheap any more.

'Procrastination is a thief of time'. This is because when you procrastinate, you lose time.

Distractions

A decision to get rid of time-killers or distractions and focus on your goals is very important and must be taken quickly but when it is delayed, time is lost. For instance a friend calls you up to hang out for a drink or two and instead of rejecting the offer so as to complete your project, you reply with "I will get back to you later." A good time manager would respond immediately with apologies and reject the offer and focus his attention on his projects. By acting with speed, he has also cancelled the second phone call that would be necessary to give his response, thus saving time. The ability to decide within 5 seconds will enable you to reclaim your lost years.

Distractions come in the form of friends and loved ones, phone calls and social media notifications.

RUN!

*Then the LORD replied: "Write down the revelation
and make it plain on tablets so that a herald may
run with it.*
HABAKKUK 2:2 NIV

According to the scriptures, God expects us to pursue
our divine calling with speed. As you read or hear the instructions of God, run with it. Begin to execute and implement it immediately. There is no room to sit and wait for
confirmation, once God has spoken, or once you discovered your calling and have written down your goals, run
with it. It is important to develop a sense of urgency concerning fulfilling your goals.

Paul was an example of a man who pursued his life's
calling with speed. He was a late entrant into the circle of
Christ's disciples and in order to redeem his lost years he
engaged the force of speed. He described his attitude to his
pursuit of his calling as a runner and a fighter. He moved
from one city to another spreading the gospel. He faced
a lot of trials and tribulations but none deterred him. He
moved with speed in order to make up for the lost years.
His speed played a significant role to his tremendous success as an apostle.

*Therefore I do not run like someone running
aimlessly; I do not fight like a boxer beating the air.*
1CORINTHIANS 9:26 NIV

Our attitude to the pursuit of our life's purpose should be that of speed and urgency.

Jesus also pursued his purpose with speed and a sense of urgency. He spent a short time on earth but he accomplished his calling because he ran with speed. Although he started his ministry at the age of thirty, he completed it at thirty-three. And within those three years, he visited a lot of towns and villages and did numerous miracles that could not be recorded for want of space. Sometimes he was on the mountain for three days teaching and preaching to the multitudes.

> *Jesus did many other things as well. If every one of them were written down, I suppose that even the whole world would not have room for the books that would be written.*
> JOHN 21:25 NIV

This level of achievement couldn't have been feasible without the force of speed. By engaging speed, you can achieve more within a shorter time and invest more value into every minute and hour of your day. You can produce more goods and services within a shorter time and you can achieve your goals and all pursuits quicker if you do it speedily. Speed therefore is an important factor in regaining your lost years.

According to my personal story which I discussed in the previous chapter, I lost many years of my academic life goofing around with friends. I was so backward academically that it earned me hard knocks on my head. But when I began to regain my lost years, I did not do it as other smart students. Having a short time to make up for many years of truancy, I worked hard and fast. My efforts paid off and within one year, I had covered the syllables of 5 years of high school. I took the exams and passed with flying colors. The power of speed can restore to you your lost years!

ORGANIZE

In order to take decisions quickly, it is important to organize your life and your daily activities. It is necessary to organize your life around your priorities and concentrate on activities that are goal-oriented.

A smart way is to plan tomorrow's activities the night before. When you know what to do and what goals to accomplish before-hand, delays are eliminated. Once you wake up, you are on the go. If you have a problem with choosing an outfit, picking out one the night before will save you a lot of time in the morning and free you to concentrate on important decisions.

Having a to-do list and working with it is a great way of cutting out distractions during the day. It is a way of de-cluttering your life and focusing on important matters. Being organized on the job will ensure that maximum value is invested into each hour of the day. Having a to-do list for the job is an excellent way to achieve more. When you prioritize your tasks for the day and tackle them starting from the most important to the least, your productivity will be increased.

WORK FAST

Speed increases our efficiency and productivity. Speed enables us to invest more value into each hour of the day. With speed, one painter can paint more houses within a specified time than another; one can read more books or complete more assignments than normally obtainable.

Daily activities must be done with speed in order to save time. This includes chores. One can learn to cook faster for instance, by planning ahead and laying out the necessary ingredients. A few adjustments in the arrangement of the kitchen itself could enhance speed thereby saving precious time. In the same vein, instead of spending the entire weekend doing laundry, cleaning or mowing the lawn, one can strategize and multi-task to save time. The saved hours can be channeled into the pursuit of goals and aspirations.

We need to discipline ourselves to think 'speed' at every point in time and in whatever we are doing. Ask yourself; "how can I do this faster"? This could mean learning to type faster on the keyboard if your work involves a lot of writing or making shorter but more straightforward phone calls or holding brief but more effective meetings.

The habit of focus which is the ability to concentrate all your attention and energy like a laser beam into the task at hand will improve your speed. This amount of concentration eliminates distractions and the resultant effect is maximum productivity. Distractions like phone calls, text messages or interruptions by people are speed-breakers. Once there is broken focus and concentration, it takes more time to recover the train of thoughts and re-establish full concentration. Without distractions, speed is increased. The habit of absolute, 100% commitment to every task at hand also increases speed.

CONCLUSION

We have established that Speed, the ability to take decisions within 5 seconds is an important principle that will enable one to accomplish more within a short time. So the question for you is how fast am I?

Do you take minor decisions quickly or do you put off them off till a later date? Are you a procrastinator? If you do not take decisions quickly, then I challenge you to start doing so. Starting with minor everyday matters for example what shirt to wear, what food to order at the restaurant, take these quickly and do not change your mind. Stick with your choice. Keep at it till it becomes a habit.

Once you develop this habit, you will be more confident and more efficient than before.

In the next chapter we will look at more principles that will help you to regain your lost years.

THE GOLDEN NUGGETS

- Speed is an important factor in regaining our lost years.

- Speed is the ability to take a decision within 5 seconds.

- To enhance our speed, we must get rid of speed-breakers like procrastination, mental laziness etc.

- Our attitude towards the fulfillment of our goals should be that of urgency and speed.

- We are to run with our vision and goals.

- Jesus and Paul fulfilled their purpose with speed.

- To gain speed, we need to organize our daily activities.

- Working with a sense of urgency will greatly increase our speed.

CHAPTER 10

SELF-EDUCATION

If a man empties his purse into his head no one can take it away from him. An investment in knowledge always pays the best interest.
BENJAMIN FRANKLIN

In this chapter, we are going to discuss the importance of education in regaining your lost years. However we will approach the issue of education from a different angle. Instead of the regular formal education we will rather discuss the importance of educating yourself by yourself.

For most people, education is over once they get their certificates. But you will learn why that attitude to education must change and why you must continue to educate yourself in your field of interest. Furthermore, you will learn ways to obtain education for yourself outside the regular classroom experience.

IMPORTANCE OF EDUCATION

The importance of education cannot be over-emphasized. An investment into any form of education will yield tremendous amounts of benefits. Education is an avenue through which we learn new skills or sharpen existing ones. It affords us the opportunity to develop our talents and turn them into marketable products. An investment into musical knowledge will produce a better artist. An investment into college degree will produce a professional.

In order to reclaim your lost years and achieve your divine purpose and calling, it is important to get educated in the line of your calling. There is no short cut to it and it cannot be circumvented. Education is important to the fulfillment of your purpose. It is mandatory to be trained in your field of endeavour. Your education may be formal or informal but is it necessary. It may be a University degree or an apprenticeship. Through education, you will be able to develop your natural talents and sharpen your skills.

Some people under-estimate the place of education in the fulfillment of their purpose. They assume natural talent is enough to achieve the success they dream about. Undeveloped natural talent will produce mediocre results. But trained and developed talent will take one to the top.

Some people can sing and because they can sing, they launch out to release an album that no one buys. Then they wonder why they failed. The great artists we listen to today especially in the Western countries train so hard as if they have no natural talent. That is why they are admired so much all over the world. They have voice trainers, dance trainers, managers and lots of coaches who ensure their skills are developed to the maximum. How do you compete with someone like that in the same industry if you have no training?

Education is about training. It is not mere acquisition of knowledge and information but ability to apply knowledge to get desired results. So self-education is about you taking it upon yourself to get specialized training in the field of your endeavor.

Self-education can be obtained through reading books, attending seminars, conferences or workshops, employing coaches and trainers, apprenticeship, mentorship programs, listening to CDs or watching on-line tutorials etc. It could be through formal education like college degrees and certification courses. It includes any avenue through which you can obtain knowledge and training to sharpen or improve your skills.

The fastest man in the world Usain Bolt, although very talented, failed woefully in his pre-Olympic events. He had to invest in self-education by hiring a personal coach and trainer. His current title as the fastest man in the world says it all. His natural talent was not enough; he needed to be trained to sprint better.

To get the best out of self-education, it is of the essence to make it structured and systematic. Draw up a learning plan with specific goals and objectives and a time-frame for achievement. Research and gather all resources you need to achieve your learning goals. Then set metrics to measure your progress. Draw up a time-table then follow your plans as though you were enrolled in a college.

OUR RAPIDLY CHANGING WORLD

We live in a constantly changing world. In fact the only thing that is constant about our world is change! Every day and in every way, our lives are constantly changing. In all fields of life, advances are being made at an amazing speed. No wonder it is called the jet age! There are lots of technological and scientific advances such that knowledge is going obsolete as new ones are emerging. It seems that every day, there are new inventions and new advances. Even the phone companies would not let you use their cell phones for more than one year! The new models are coming out so fast that before you realize what is happening, your 2 year old phone is tagged obsolete. The car companies no longer release a new model after three to four years as before, rather new models with new features and amazing artificial intelligence are bombarding us every year! It is really tough to keep up with today's technological speed.

The Information Technology industry changes every day it seems! Daily we are bombarded with new apps and inventions that it is difficult to keep up with them. There are upgrades on our PC operating system almost every day. New apps are developed and old ones are upgraded every day. Just a few years ago, there was nothing like Facebook or Twitter but today, social media has completely taken over our lives. If you are not active in any, you might as well be in the dark ages! And if your business or organization is not active on social media, the same applies.

In the healthcare industry, the past decade has brought about so many new advances, new medications, new diagnostic tools and procedures, new regulations etc. that if one is not up to date, he would not be able to perform optimally. A Pharmacist who is relying on the knowledge he gained ten years ago in Pharmacy school will not be able to counsel patients on the new medicines, side effects or drug interactions. His knowledge has become obsolete and his relevance has declined.

The same goes with a physician who is ignorant of the latest electronic interventions in the diagnosis and treatment of certain diseases. Since he does not employ these tools, he is inadvertently denying his patients of the best medical intervention. And if he is unaware that there are new medications with fewer or milder side effects, he may continue to prescribe the old ones thereby exposing his patients to the dangers of the medication. His ignorance of the current knowledge in his field may cost him money in addition to loss of his clients or his medical license in the long run.

A farmer who is not up to date with the happenings in his field of agriculture may continue with his methods of operation whereas there are better ways to get things done. He may not enjoy the full benefits of mechanized farming which ought to make him more productive. Secondly he may be planting a particular species of crops not knowing that there is a new and improved version that is resistant to the prevalent pest and diseases in his locality. The resultant effect: reduced profitability.

An organization or a company which is not up to date with the current trends in the market may go out of business. But knowing the current trend and modeling their business after it will ensure that they remain in the market and be profitable. For instance, just a few years ago typists and typewriters were in business. To get any document written necessitated a typist and a typewriter to get the job done. Companies and organizations hired typists and invested in typewriters. Both the typists and the makers of the typewriters were making good money. However, both have become so obsolete that today's teenagers are ignorant of them.

In this computer/internet age, basic knowledge of the computer is not an option anymore. It is a necessity. Previously, during job interviews, one could be asked if they had basic computer knowledge, but that question is equally becoming obsolete. It is assumed that they have it. Computer skills have become as basic as having the educational qualification for the job.

In today's world everything is changing and we must keep up with information especially in our field of endeavor in order to remain relevant and worthwhile. And the way to do so is through self-education. This can be done by reading articles, attending conferences, subscribing to publications and magazines and searching the internet for new information.

FORMAL EDUCATION IS NOT ENOUGH

There's always room for improvement, you know —
it's the biggest room in the house.
LOUISE HEATH LEBER

A lot of people stop their education once they obtain their diploma or degree certificates from higher institutions. But is a college certificate enough to keep you relevant and enable you fulfill your goals? The answer as you can easily deduce is "No." Formal education is very important for the fulfillment of your goals but it is not enough. It is only a stepping stone because it gives you the needed foundation to enable you continue with self-education. After formal education is over, self-education commences.

In order to regain your lost years, it is important to have some form of formal education in the area of your calling. This will set your foundation and teach you the basics about your field of interest. For instance, if your goal is to be a teacher, then it would profit you immensely to get a formal training in teaching. A university degree or college diploma would train you on the rudiments of becoming a teacher. It will expose you to teaching skills; types of students and their temperaments and the teaching methods appropriate for students of various ages. Learning under an authority in the field i.e. the professors and lecturers will give you an opportunity to ask questions and tap into their wealth of knowledge.

Learning under a systematic and structured environment with laid-down curriculum will provide you all you need to function in that field. For example, after a 4-year university program, an Accountant can confidently work as one; same goes for any professional. Thus formal education is enough to get you started in your chosen field. You can get hired or start your own business based on the specialized knowledge obtained through the University. But in order to remain relevant, achieve more and regain your lost years, it is imperative to go further and educate yourself. To get started, a formal education is required but to sustain growth, relevance and mastery, self-education is needful.

ADVANTAGES OF SELF-EDUCATION

*If you are planning for a year, sow rice; if you
are planning for a decade, plant trees; if you are
planning for a lifetime, educate people.*
CHINESE PROVERB

The benefits of education last for a lifetime. Therefore every investment into acquiring knowledge is not a waste. These are some of the benefits of self-education.

Personal Development

Self-Education is about taking personal responsibility to improve your knowledge-base in any field of your desire. Today, access to knowledge is only a click away. With computers, the internet and search engines like Google, all the information you need is at your fingertips. Therefore the absence of a well-equipped library is not a limitation anymore. These days there are lots of self-taught individuals. By using self-help videos on YouTube, people have learnt skills which have made them rich. From culinary skills to writing, speaking skills or money skills, almost everything can be found online.

Increased productivity

Self-education is about adding value to yourself via the acquisition of more knowledge so as to increase your worth. As your value is increased, your productivity is increased. As you know more, your performance is improved and your output is increased. And your overall effectiveness is increased. A baker who has sharpened his skills will bake better, bake more and increase his profits more than an un-educated baker.

A self-educated hotelier will manage his hotel, hire better staff, maintain an excellent customer service and provide excellent meals for his customers. This is because he has invested time to educate himself on all aspects of the hospitality industry and has gained knowledge from the experts in his field. He has also stayed relevant and up to date as per the current trends in the business. But a fellow colleague who has not educated himself in any form will have challenges operating his hotel and will not attain the same level of success.

Through self-education you can develop your money skills and learn how to save, invest and grow your wealth. By reading books on money management and especially those written by authorities in the field or by attending seminars and workshops, you can acquire money skills. These skills are not taught in the higher institutions so you can only access it through self-education.

Self-discovery

Through self-education you can discover who you really are; your potentials, capabilities and latent talents and develop them. Through self-education, you can unravel and develop innate talents. I met a gentleman who is an Engineer. Although he had a very good job with the government, he began to pursue his passion for stocks and shares. He trained himself to be a stockbroker by soaking up all information he could lay his hands on. He became very good at trading stocks, options etc that he began to teach his colleagues and friends. He became so successful that he quit his job to pursue his passion.

Your potentials are not defined by whatever career you studied in the University. It is limitless. You can become anything you want to be! All you need is to get the training in that field. The 'you' that you see is not all there is to you. There is so much more to you. The unknown you can make you very successful if you will discover and develop it through education. You can earn more money and live a better quality of life by self-education.

Increased Net-worth

Self-education is about increasing your net-worth by spreading your tentacles and widening your scope of knowledge. Though self-education, you can gain knowledge in any field of interest. I know a young man who was working as a sales person in a retail shop a few years ago earning about fifteen thousand dollars annually. Then he heard that someone was giving free tutorials on Quality Assurance, a branch of Information Technology. He decided to attend simply out of curiosity. After the course, he prepared his résumé and submitted it. He got hired at a salary of sixty thousand dollars per annum. Three years later, he moved to a new job still in IT that offered him one hundred and five thousand dollars.

Increased Influence

Apostle Paul of the bible was a lawyer by profession. He received formal education in law. According to the scriptures, he was trained by Gamaliel, one of the best instructors in his time. Paul, like the other apostles was not trained as a Pharisee or Sadducees, the official teachers of the biblical laws. But after his conversion, Paul engaged himself fully into self-education in biblical matters. He went into deep research, reading all manner of written works. He had parchments, scrolls, i.e. books and written works which he studied.

> *When you come, bring the cloak that I left with*
> *Carpus at Troas, and my scrolls, especially*
> *the parchments.*
> 2 TIMOTHY 4:13 NIV

His depth of knowledge enabled him to challenge the Pharisees and Sadducees with accuracy. In the book of Acts of the apostles, Paul argued and defended his religious beliefs and convictions without a myopic view. His research had exposed him to a wide range of knowledge and information and made his arguments informed and convincing.

Self-education was also responsible for his prolific writings. He wrote over two-thirds of the New Testament. And his writings were full of deep truths and well-articulated arguments about controversial topics prevailing in the time. It is easy to detect his legal training in the style of his letters.

Paul developed himself by himself. Although his legal training provided the launch pad and enabled him to write, he discovered more through his self-education. He expanded his scope of influence and did more exploit than his fellow apostles.

BECOME A READER

Employ your time in improving yourself by other men's writings so that you shall come easily by what others labored hard for.
SOCRATES

Reading is a major way to engage in self-education. Reading books is a major avenue to develop and improve yourself. Any investment in books is a huge and worthwhile investment. Reading books affords you the priceless opportunity to enjoy information others labored hard to discover. It gives you the opportunity to learn from the experiences of others without paying any price for it. Reading the works of others is an opportunity to meet great people and listen to their words of wisdom. Reading also affords you the opportunity to meet giants and achievers in your field of endeavour and stand on their shoulders.

Reading is a cheap way to train yourself without paying the author for a private session. Imagine what it would cost you to hire the author for one hour compared to the price of his book? You may not afford to pay Barack Obama for one hour but by reading his book, you have hired him to speak to you for a token.

Whatever your field of interest is, when you read books written by the giants in that field you will acquire their knowledge and practical wisdom. This will get you further faster than your contemporaries. If your field is entrepreneurship, find out the successful ones in the field, those whom you admire, who have achieved great success, read everything they have written about business and investment and learn from them. Practice their suggestions and pieces of advice; copy their styles and patterns and as you do what they did, you will achieve success.

Reading ought to be one of your hobbies. Reading one book per week is an excellent goal to set. This will accumulate to fifty-two books by the end of the year. You will not think on the same level as someone who has read only one book throughout the year. Knowledge, they say is power, therefore through books, you gain power, greatness and success.

SELF-EDUCATION WITH SPEED, FOCUS AND INTENSITY

We have established the importance of self-education towards the realization of our goals. But in order to regain your lost years, it is vital to invest into self-education with Speed, Focus and Intensity.

This means that educating yourself in the area of your calling should not be done as normal. Instead you need to combine these qualities in the process of self-education. All activities targeted to the training and development of your potentials must be done with Speed, Focus and Intensity. You must invest heavily into improving yourself in your field, sharpening your skills in order to maintain relevance. No amount of money or time is too much to invest in your education. It is an investment that will yield good interest.

If you think education is expensive, try ignorance.
ANDY MCINTYRE

Although it is great to be a versatile reader, you must be focused to read in your field for one hour every day. This will keep you up to date as per the newest developments and establish your relevance in the industry. As you invest an hour every day, you will not only keep abreast of the latest, you will also widen your scope of knowledge and gain mastery in your field.

Engage the power of focus into your personal development in your field. For instance, if your calling is to be beautician, concentrate on it till you become an authority in that field and can tell the latest trends in the market. Develop it to such levels that people can consult you on matters of beauty.

The process of self-education must be done with speed and a sense of urgency in order to reclaim lost time. Distraction and speed killers must be eliminated.

Finally self-education must be done with intensity. The Asians are to be emulated in this regards. There needs to be an extreme form of energy, drive and enthusiasm targeted towards training oneself to be the best in his or her chosen field. Self-education must be done in a systematic manner and the focus must be on obtaining tangible results within the shortest time. The quality of Intensity makes a person to be result-oriented and goal-oriented. Therefore intensity will ensure that maximum value is derived from self-education.

The combination of these qualities in the process of self-education will facilitate greater results within a shorter time.

CONCLUSION

Now you have seen the importance of self-education and its relevance to regaining your lost years. As usual the question is how can you apply this knowledge in your life?

Are you current regarding the recent advances in your field of endeavor? Are you up to date with the advances in info tech with reference to your chosen field? Are you utilizing the educational resources available online to the maximum especially the free ones?

Instead of wasting your precious time on social media, divert those hours into keeping up with your career or profession. Sharpen your knowledge and improve on your skillset. It could be your computer literacy or your professional skills. Take advantage of tutorials and free videos to develop yourself and increase your worth.

In addition, if you are not a reader, become one! You can either read it or listen to the audio version. But you must discipline yourself to read at least one book each month.

In the next chapter, we will discuss another interesting principle which many have relegated to the background. This principle is a very vital key to redeeming your lost years in any aspect of your life.

THE GOLDEN NUGGETS

- Education is important in reclaiming our lost years.

- Our world is rapidly changing and to remain relevant, we need to engage in self-education.

- Formal education is not enough, self-education starts where formal education stops.

- Through self-education, we develop our potentials and make them commercially relevant.

- Through self-education we widen our scope of knowledge and embrace new information.

- Through self-education, we increase our worth and add value to our lives.

- Our productivity and scope of influence are increased through self-education.

- Reading should become your hobby.

- Self-education should be done systematically with set goals and objectives.

- Self-education should be done with Speed, Focus and Intensity in order to reclaim your lost years.

CHAPTER 11

CONVERSION THROUGH HARD WORK

We have discussed the importance of time and ways of regaining our time from time-killers. Now we shall discuss how to utilize the saved hours and convert them into valuable goods or services. In this chapter we will discuss the principle of time conversion and the means or tools of conversion. We shall discuss the misconceptions surrounding this principle especially among some Pentecostals. But most importantly, we will discuss biblical view of this principle as well as the advantages of incorporating it as a part of our lifestyle.

CONVERSION OF TIME

Life is about Conversion. This means that life is about converting time into valuable products to enrich our lives and the lives of others. Time is our greatest resource as earlier discussed. It is the greatest gift the creator blessed us with. Time is more valuable than money because money is made through time but time cannot be bought with money.

We have also discussed that time cannot be saved but can be harnessed and converted into one product or another. For instance, time was harnessed in a car factory by the workers and that time was used to build a car. Time was harnessed by the architect and builders and the hours were used to construct a house.

Everything is made out of time. A medical degree is a product of time. Eight or more years were converted through University Education to produce a medical doctor. Another eight years or less could be converted to produce a Lawyer or a Geologist or any other professional. So we become anything through the power of conversion. We can convert time into valuable products in our lives. You can become anything by converting your time into whatever you desire to be. Once you discover your calling or your purpose, you need to convert every hour into becoming it.

The principle of conversion enables us to maximize time. When time is not converted into a valuable product, it is lost. So it is important to harness and convert every single minute of the day into valuable goods or services. Take three young men riding the bus to work for example. The first man is simply enjoying the one hour commute, looking out of the window, assessing other passengers; their appearances and fashion style etc.

The second passenger is listening to an audio book and jotting down some notes on his journal while the last man is writing an article for his blog. During the one-hour commute, these men have converted their time into both useful and useless goods. The first man did not produce any tangible goods or services. He wasted one hour of his life. However the other men enriched their lives by the goods they produced. The second man added value to himself and last man developed a valuable product that will enhance some else's life.

Two ladies are in a salon getting their beauty treatments. The first lady, while getting her manicure and hair done is conversing with the salon workers on the last celebrity news in town, the latest fashion trend and the popular gist on social media. The second lady however, has her earpiece on listening to a motivational speech on time management. Both ladies converted their two-hour salon time into different products. One added value but the other did not.

Regaining your lost years is about converting your time into your goals and life's purpose.

WORK, A TOOL FOR CONVERSION

Work is the most important tool for conversion of time into valuable products and services. It is work that enables us to convert time into whatever we desire. Time is our greatest treasure whereas work is greatest tool for conversion of time into valuable products. Both time and work are gifts from God to make our lives better.

Work is the greatest instrument to discover that there is a seed of greatness in you; you are here to fulfill a divine mandate and you are well-equipped for it. There are hidden abilities inside of you that will only be unraveled through work. That's the beauty of work. It is an avenue to discover who you really are and the amazing possibilities within you.

Through working as a slave and a prisoner, Joseph discovered the greatness inside of him. The bible tells in Genesis chapter 38 how as a young lad, Joseph was so loved by his father that his brothers hated him and sold him into slavery. While working as a slave for Potiphar, his leadership skills were discovered and nurtured. And his master placed him in charge of his entire household. Later on, based on a false accusation, he was imprisoned and there, his leadership and managerial skills were further groomed. He was assigned as the head of the prisoners and he ran the entire prison. He was in charge of his fellow prisoners and was responsible for smooth operation of the prison.

Eventually when he was released by Pharaoh and made the Prime Minister of the land of Egypt, he excelled. Through his work experiences, he had been groomed and prepared for the assignment. Through work he discovered his leadership, supervisory and managerial skills and honed them to the point of mastery.

Through work, our innate gifts and talents are converted to commercially viable skills. Our potentials are developed through work to be marketable. And through work our goals and visions will be accomplished.

Great artists were not born great; they developed their talents to a degree that it made them great. For instance, Michelangelo, the famous Italian artist still considered the greatest artist of all times said: *"If people knew how hard I had to work to gain my mastery, it would not seem so wonderful at all."*

He had to work hard to develop his talent and make it of great worth. Michelangelo was such a hard worker, he would go into solitude for months to work on a projects. Day in, day out, he was either painting or chiseling away at a piece of rock to create masterpieces that remain works of ingenuity today. According to his quote, hard work was the secret to his mastery. One would have assumed that he was simply gifted, but natural gifting are not enough to turn you into a success, it must be developed. Work is an avenue to do so.

WORK A GIFT FROM GOD

Work is a gift from God which enables us to convert time into valuable resources. God instituted work. A lot of people including some Christians cringe at work. They assume that work is a curse. No, not at all! Work is neither a curse nor the result of the curse in the Garden of Eden.

God instituted work before the fall of man. In the book of Genesis we are told that:

> *The Lord God took the man and put him in the Garden of Eden to work it and take care of it.*
> GENESIS 2:15 NIV

After God created Adam, he instructed him to work and keep the Garden of Eden. This happened before God created Eve and before the fall of man. It is surprising that God didn't make the apples to fall off the tree for Adam rather he instructed him to work and maintain the garden. A lot of people would have expected God to place Adam in the garden without any responsibilities or any form of labor. But the bible says "*The one who is unwilling to work shall not eat.*" (2 Thessalonians 3:10 NIV).

So work is God's invention and it is a good thing because everything God created is good. Work is good because it is a tool that empowers us to discover the hidden treasures inside us. Through work, you can unravel your potentials and the deposits God planted in you. Work is to be enjoyed because it offers us an opportunity to maximize our potentials and find out who we really are.

Through work, you will discover hidden abilities and you will be amazed at the potentials you didn't realize you had. So to regain your lost years, you must utilize the tool of work to convert time into your goals and purpose.

Some Christians believe that God is no longer working. They assume that because God rested on the seventh day, he is still resting and therefore work is not a good thing. Although the scriptures states that God ended the creation on the sixth day and rested on the seventh, God is still working.

> *In his defense Jesus said to them, "My Father is always at his work to this very day, and I too am working."*
> JOHN 5:17 NIV

God therefore is always working. He is still busy working, healing the sick, raising the dead, answering the prayers of his saints. Work enables God to reveals aspects of his personality hitherto unknown. For instance, when God raises the dead, he becomes known as a life-giver. When he delivers from dangerous or impossible situations, He becomes known as a deliverer and when he heals the sick, he is called a healer.

Jesus worked very hard while on earth. In fact he worked so hard that he would forgo food despite being famished and exhausted, in order to complete the project at hand. Jesus put work before food and other personal comfort.

In the book of John, Jesus and his disciples arrived at the city of Samaria. He was so hungry and exhausted that his disciples left him by a well and went into the city to purchase food. However, on their return, they met him preaching the gospel to a lady. He refused to eat till his work was completed.

> *Jacob's well was there, and Jesus, tired as he was from the journey, sat down by the well. It was about noon. When a Samaritan woman came to draw water, Jesus said to her, "Will you give me a drink?" (His disciples had gone into the town to buy food.).... Meanwhile his disciples urged him, "Rabbi, eat something. But he said to them, "I have food to eat that you know nothing about. Then his disciples said to each other, "Could someone have brought him food?" "My food," said Jesus, "is to do the will of him who sent me and to finish his work.*
> JOHN 4: 6-7; 31-34 NIV

Jesus was committed to working and completing his assignment despite his physical needs. He was passionate and intense about work. This should be the attitude of everyone especially Christians.

Although the Lord Jesus had ascended into heaven, according to the bible, he is still working. In the book of Mark, the bible records that as the disciples went out to work for Jesus, he accompanied them, working with them through the signs and wonders that took place.

Then the disciples went out and preached everywhere, and the Lord worked with them and confirmed his word by the signs that accompanied it.
MARK 16:20 NIV

God is still working, Jesus is still working and the Holy Spirit is still working therefore it is wrong to assume otherwise. Work therefore is a good thing.

WORK NOT JOB

Work is an invention from God, but a job is not. God expects us to work but not in a job.

Then people go out to their work, to their labor until evening.
PSALM 104:23NIV

God expects man to do his own work. What does that mean? Man's work is the place of his calling and purpose. God created us all for a reason, for a purpose and that is where he expects us to work and develop. Work is supposed to be in your own area of calling. We have discussed the importance of discovering our purpose in life. God expects you to bring forth fruit in your own area of calling. He expects us to till the ground of our calling.

For instance, if God's calling in your life is to be a nurse, he expects you till the ground of nursing. He expects you to touch lives and make an impact through nursing. So when you work as a nurse, you are fulfilling your calling.

However, anything man does that is outside of his calling is a job. When you are working outside of your purpose, it is a job. If your calling is to be a teacher but you are working as a nurse, that is a job. The difference between both nurses is that one is called by God to be a nurse while the other is in nursing simply to make money.

For instance, many Nigerians who migrate abroad especially the US abandon their professions or callings and become nurses for financial reasons. Because the job is easily available and pays reasonably well, a lot of them flood into the nursing career. You see a lot of lawyers, accountants and entrepreneurs working as nurses in the hospital. If they did this for short-term purposes while developing their own career, it is Ok, but most times, they get stuck in the rut. Year in and year out, they are slaving away, working passionlessly for a job instead of developing their calling.

If you find yourself in a job, don't stay there permanently. Discover your purpose and begin to invest some hours daily into developing it. And at the proper time, make a smooth transition from the job to your work.

Your greatness is buried in your calling and your purpose. And through the tool of hard work, you can discover and unravel that greatness. God has placed seeds of greatness in each of us. But the key lies in discovering our purpose and tilling the ground because therein lies those seeds.

Greatness cannot be achieved outside of your purpose despite the height of success you attain. A beautiful flower vase could be used to store water. But no matter the volume of water it stores, it has failed in its purpose. Its work is to hold a bouquet of flowers. Success therefore is only attainable in your calling. Your success is buried in your work. Discover your calling and strive for greatness through work.

In order to reclaim our lost years, we must use the tool of work to convert time into our goals and dreams.

WORK HARD AND LONG

Work is our most important tool of conversion. Through hard work, we can convert the harnessed time into becoming the person we were created to be. The importance of work cannot be over-emphasized.

A dream doesn't become a reality through magic; it takes sweat, determination and hard work.
Colin Powel

Our dreams and goals will not materialize if we are unwilling to work hard. It takes burning the midnight oil to become a successful student. It takes hard work i.e. reading, researching and staying up late at night to complete assignments and projects to become a successful student.

It takes hard work to be a master in every field of endeavor. There is no success story without the price of hard work attached to it. You must be willing to work hard so as to make your dreams come to pass. When you work hard in your area of calling, it is a good investment. You can become the best if you pay the price of hard work.

Hard work is scriptural. God wants us to work hard, because he hates laziness. According to the book of Psalm:

Then people go out to their work, to their labor until evening.
PSALM 104:23 NIV

According to the dictionary, labor means physical or mental work, especially of a hard or fatiguing kind. It means toil, hard work, to strive and exert oneself. Thus God expects us to toil, work hard, and exert ourselves in the pursuit of our goals. So this should be our work ethics, and our attitude to work. The concept of success falling onto our laps like ripe apples off the apple tree is a lie. We must labor in our area of calling in order to accomplish it and achieve greatness.

Successful achievers have a common denominator; hard work. To be a success in life, get rid of the mentality of laziness and embrace hard work. Nothing great comes easy in life. Be ready to work hard in order to make your life a success. Fall in love with hard work and it will unlock all the greatness in you.

Successful people are not gifted; they just work hard, then succeed on purpose.
G.K. NIELSON

Hard work will restore to you, your lost years. It will deliver your goals and make you a success in life.

Debunk the philosophy that you can make it without hard work. The only place where success comes before work is in the dictionary. But in this real world, you have to pay the price of hard work before you can achieve success in any goal.

There is no substitute for hard work.
THOMAS EDISON

God instituted labor in our place of calling i.e. in our purpose. When you labor in your work, it will not be a strenuous investment instead you will enjoy it. You will not notice the passage of time while working. It will be refreshing and enjoyable. But when you labor in a job, it will be drudgery and herculean. This is the why you must ensure that you are engaged in your God-ordained purpose.

There is a popular footballer who says that he enjoys playing football. He could play football any time of the day. But his amazement is that he gets paid for doing something he loves. This is not unique to that footballer. Most people who are in their work enjoy what they do so much that getting paid is an added bonus.

Imagine paying Mark Zuckerberg to write software codes! You are paying him for his hobby because writing codes is more fun than work to him. When you discover your purpose, working to accomplish it would be like a hobby to you.

WORK LONG

Then people go out to their work, to their labor until evening.
PSALM 104:23 NIV

Man is expected to labor until the evening; however some people work till late afternoon and pack up their bags. But the scriptures say that work is till evening.

Evening means the period of time at the end of the day, usually from about 6p.m. to bedtime. This translates to more than eight hours of hard work! Therefore God expects us to work hard and long in our field. This instruction will only seem strenuous to one working in a job for salary. But when you are doing something you love, you will not notice the passage of time. Your attention will be so captivated that you will naturally work hard and long.

Discover your calling and work hard and long in it and your lost years will be restored back to you.

The story was told of a famous scientist who was so passionate, intense and focused on his experiments that he lost count of time. It was said that on one occasion he got into his laboratory on Monday morning and locked himself in. By 2 pm on Friday his concerned colleagues broke down the door to his laboratory. He complained about their forced entry claiming he just got into the laboratory and the time was 2 pm. But they told him that it was 2 pm of Friday, not Monday!

He didn't notice the passage of time due to the depth of his focus and concentration. Neither did he notice or feel hunger pangs. He didn't eat anything except drink water.

Most successful people work hard and long. They are so in love with their work, it is not farfetched to call them workaholics. They work more than eight hours daily. In fact, most successful people work between 12 to 18 hours daily. Since they are already successful, why do they work so hard you may ask? One may expect millionaires or billionaires to spend their time relaxing on a beach, basking in the warmth of the Caribbean sun yet they are stuck in their offices working like Trojan. Isn't wealth accumulation the reason for hard work? Most successful people are driven by the love and passion for their work, not necessarily the money. They may start off with a goal to achieve success and financial freedom but as they succeed, they are consumed with a passion for work that not working seems abnormal to them.

However, the opposite is seen among the poor who spend hours watching the TV and are too lazy to work hard. They depend on government benefits where available. Some people do better and put in eight hours of work daily which translates to mediocre results. To be very successful and regain your lost years, you need to work like successful people do.

Personally I work between 18 to 20 hours every day. There is a lot to be accomplished and 24 hours is not enough! As a result, I am able to achieve a lot and I enjoy what I do.

According to a study on the sleep habits of 21 highly successful people in history, it was discovered that majority of them slept for only 4 to 6 hours daily1. This gave them more hours to invest into their work.

THE 10,000 HOURS RULE

In the book *Outliers*, author Malcolm Gladwell says that it takes roughly ten thousand hours of practice to achieve mastery in a field. Gladwell studied the lives of very successful people including Bill Gates, the Beatles and concluded that their success was not due to natural talents but as a result of long hours of practice. According to his findings, Bill Gates had spent thousands upon thousands of hours practicing on the computer. He practiced in school and in addition, he would sneak out at night to write codes at the nearby University. So at the time he quit college to start his company, he was no novice. He had invested more hours into writing computer programs than his contemporaries.

The same was true of the Beatles. Before they came into international limelight, they had spent hours and years playing and developing their skills in smaller clubs. At the time of their international exposure, they had invested more hours in their career than any of their contemporaries.

If this principle is true then it means that 10,000 hours of practice in any field will make you a master. You can be exceptional and achieve world class success in that career if you invest 10,000 hours of quality work in it.

This translates to four hours of hard work in your career every day. It will make you a master and among the world best in 10 years. Eight hours of hard work in your field daily will deliver the same result in 5 years. That is the reason to ensure that you are working in your calling, you will achieve mastery faster.

If you are working at a job so as to make ends meet, that is Ok. But carve out three to four hours every day and invest in your real calling /purpose. And while at it, invest the qualities of Focus, Speed and Intensity into your work, you will produce tremendous results

LAZINESS

Go to the ant, you sluggard; consider its ways and be wise! It has no commander, no overseer or ruler, yet it stores its provisions in summer and gathers its food at harvest. How long will you lie there, you sluggard? When will you get up from your sleep? A little sleep, a little slumber, a little folding of the hands to rest — and poverty will come on you like a thief and scarcity like an armed man.

PROVERBS 6:6-11 NIV

The Holy Bible has a lot to say about laziness. Here it admonishes a lazy person to learn from the ants about wisdom and hard work. Laziness will reduce one to poverty and scarcity. But hard work will bring wealth and prosperity. For instance some students prefer to live a life of ease rather than paying the price of diligence by studying their books. They prefer to play hard instead of work hard. They attend parties all weekend or they travel out of the campuses to visit their friends and after the examination, their performances will tell the tale. The results of their actions are not only apparent immediately, but also in the future.

There is no substitute for hard work.

THOMAS EDISON

According to Edison, nothing can take the place of hard work in achieving success in any venture. However many people do not realize this important truth. Instead they venture to substitute hard work with a lot of things like luck, praying, fasting, anointing or sowing seeds. But none of these can take the place of hard work because God ordained it to be so.

Work is God's invention and it is an avenue to achieve success in the place of our gifting. Although God blesses us with special gifts and abilities, he has purposed that those gifts will be commercially viable through hard work. Thus a musically gifted person has to work hard at training the voice before people will pay to hear him. Without hard work, it yields no gains.

A lot of people do not understand the importance of hard work. They are deceived by easy money. They envy people who are born with the silver spoon and wish they had their good fortune. They imagine that wealth is restricted to some special people due to their origin or family ties. What they have failed to understand is that hard work will produce the same results for them. There are numerous rags to riches stories to prove that. And there are evidences that prove that without the discipline of work, some offspring of the rich lose all the wealth bequeathed to them.

You can achieve success despite your background. You must not have a royal lineage or be born into the families of generational wealth to be a success financially. Neither do you need to be born into a family of academic erudite to become one. The important thing is to discover your calling and invest your time and energy into it.

According to Forbes list of world richest, nearly two-thirds of the 1,810 entrants on Forbes' 2016 World's Billionaires list are self-made entrepreneurs who started with little more than a vision and some savings and hard work. They include Bill Gates, Mark Zuckerberg of Facebook, Amazon's Jeff Bezos etc.

Others believe that success is as a result of luck so they try their luck at getting rich by playing the lottery or by engaging in casino. A lot have wasted their money in such ventures and some have committed suicide.

Some ignorantly resort to playing the lottery in order to be rich. But statistics show that after a few years, most lottery winners lose everything they won and some were worse off than before the big win. In fact, many people's lives became notably worse after they got super rich, and they managed to lose it all quite quickly.

William Post won $16,2 million in the Pennsylvania lottery in 1988 but was $1 million in debt within a year. He ultimately filed for bankruptcy, and faced a stint in jail for firing a gun at a bill collector.

Unlike these lottery winners, millionaires who went bankrupt at one time or the other during their career managed to re-apply their skills and through hard work recovered their wealth and multiplied it e.g. Henry Ford.

Others especially some Pentecostals are ignorant of the laws of financial prosperity and do not appreciate the importance of hard work as a means of achieving financial success. They would rather spend hours in church, praying, fasting and quoting scriptures so as to be successful. As we have seen earlier, God instituted hard work as a means of achieving success in our areas of calling.

There is a place of prayers in fulfilling your calling and purpose but it cannot take the place the hard work. It is possible to achieve success without prayers but impossible to achieve success without hard work. Some of the most successful and wealthiest people in the world are not even Christians while some are atheists. But they are successful in their fields of endeavor.

These Christians need to put on their overalls and begin to labor in their calling in order to become successful. The prayers and fasting will not take the place of hard work.

Some Pentecostals spend a lot of time in church meetings or programs so as to receive anointing for prosperity instead of working and tilling the ground of their calling. No wonder they do not see much success. The place of hard work cannot be substituted with church programs or anointing services.

Jesus is the son of God. He was also anointed with the Holy Spirit during his life on earth. Yet he was a hard worker, forgoing food and personal comfort while working. Jesus was also very prayerful. According to the scriptures, he would spend the entire night praying in the mountains. Yet he worked very hard to achieve success in his calling. The anointing, his sonship and his prayerfulness did not make him relegate hard work to the background. But Pentecostals would prefer to get the anointing that would produce success rather than work hard. The place of labor cannot be substituted with the anointing or prayers.

Paul the apostle was an anointed man of God. He was so anointed that he wrote about two-thirds of the New Testament. He was also a man of prayers. He told the Corinthian church that he prayed more than all of them. *"I thank God that I speak in tongues more than all of you."* (1Corinthians 14:18 NIV)

Despite being a man of prayers and a highly anointed man, he worked hard. In fact, he stated that he worked more than the rest of the apostles.

> *But by the grace of God I am what I am, and his grace to me was not without effect. No, I worked harder than all of them — yet not I, but the grace of God that was with me*
>
> 1 CORINTHIANS 15:10 NIV

He did not substitute the place of hard work with prayers or the anointing. Paul was a workaholic and he attributed his success in ministry to his hard work rather than his gifts or anointing.

> *Do you see someone skilled in their work? They will serve before kings; they will not serve before officials of low rank.*
>
> PROVERBS 22:29 NIV

Hard work will take you places in life. It will raise you to stand before kings and great people. Promotion comes with hard work. It is impossible to be diligent and work hard and remain poor. Success will come to the man who works hard for it.

WORK WITH FOCUS, SPEED
AND INTENSITY

We have established the importance of hard work as a tool to achieve success in our field of endeavour. However because you are in a race against time, trying to regain your lost years, hard work alone will not suffice. It has to be combined with the qualities of Focus, Speed and Intensity.

These three qualities must be present as you work on your goals and visions. As earlier said, the key to reclaiming your lost years is to load the maximum amount of value into every hour of the day. By combining these three qualities, you will be able to invest maximum value into every hour of work.

When work is done with Focus and Concentration, all distractions are by-passed and more value is produced for every hour of work. Concentrate on any task at hand and avoid distractions from people or things. For instance while working, put your phone on silent mode and avoid checking your social media while working on the computer. Reduce human interruptions as much as possible.

Working with focus entails being organized; not jumping from one task to another. Rather, bringing each to completion before starting another. It also means to prioritize your tasks; working on the most important before the less important. Focus ensures maximum input of your energy and attention and gives more results for your labour.

To regain your lost years, it is also important to engage the quality of Speed. Work with speed and develop a sense of urgency in handling every task. However the quality of your work must not be sacrificed for speed. Take quick decisions and avoid procrastinations on work-related matters.

Work with intensity: Work with an extreme form of enthusiasm, energy and drive. Work with lots of passion and zeal. Be intense about the task before you. Work at it to obtain result i.e. be result-driven. Work to achieve your set goals.

CONCLUSION

Having seen the importance and beauty of work, I bet you have changed your negative attitude towards it and have fallen in love with work. Hard work is a gift from God. It is not a curse as some presume; instead it is an avenue to realize your goals and visions. Work is good, it is a treasure, and it is something to be desired and not to be frowned upon.

With this new understanding about work, I urge you to begin to work like never before. First, increase the number of hours you invest in your goals. Become a workaholic doing what you love and what God has called you to do. Do not listen to mockers or naysayers since you know better. Use work to discover who you are and the hidden potentials you have.

Secondly, work with focus, speed and intensity. Concentrate fully on any task before you and give it your best. Avoid distractions while working. Turn off or put electronic gadgets on silent mode and give your assignments the best of your abilities.

In the next chapter I will introduce yet another powerful principle that will enable you harness large portions of time which you can invest into. It is a practice that will eliminate distractions or keep it at the barest minimum.

THE GOLDEN NUGGETS

- Work is the most important tool for conversion of time into valuable goods and services.

- Work was instituted by God before the fall of Adam; therefore it is not a curse but a blessing.

- God is still working and Jesus is also working therefore we must work.

- Work is a tool to discover the hidden treasures, potentials and abilities inside us.

- Work is God's invention but job is not. Work is in our area of calling whereas a job is a means of survival outside of our divine calling.

- God expects us to labor and work long and hard in our calling.

- There is no success without hard work

- Laziness will only lead to poverty and scarcity.

- There is no substitute for hard work, not even luck or anointing or sowing seeds.

- To reclaim our lost years, work must be combined with the qualities of Focus, Speed and Intensity.

CHAPTER 12

POWER OF SOLITUDE

Regaining our lost years is a fight against time. As earlier explained, time is ticking and we need to capture it and invest maximum value into it. The greater the amount of time we are able to capture, the more value we can invest. That is the reason why we have learnt to say 'No' to time killers in chapter 3.

In this chapter, we will discuss a powerful practice that will enable you to harness a large chunk of your time and invest maximum value into it so as to produce more results. It is called Solitude.

Solitude is defined as a state of being alone, usually because you want to be. It also means to be in seclusion or isolation. Solitude is a time of complete separation from everybody and everything else to be alone with you.

SOLITUDE

Solitude which is a time of separation to be alone is a tool that will enable us to maximize our time. Through solitude, we can harness more hours of the day and invest maximum and concentrated value into them. Solitude is like grabbing the bulls of time by the horns, taking an aggressive stance against the loss of our time and making the most of it.

The practice of solitude can be likened to the process of concentrating light rays through a laser into a single but powerful beam. Through solitude, we can concentrate time and convert it into more valuable goods. During solitude, the entire 24 hours of the day is yours and yours alone. No one and nothing is competing with you.

I practice solitude. For the last eighteen years of my life, I have practiced solitude every single month. I lock myself away from everything and everybody including my wife and children. Without any phone, TV or even food, I stay in solitude for about three to seven days to develop myself, organize my life, spend quality time with God or produce any product that I desire. Without any distraction, I am fully focused on whatever goal I want to achieve. Because I am extremely focused and concentrated on my goals, my speed triples and I produce more results than before.

Solitude helps us to overcome distractions. In life, a lot of things compete for our attention and these may include family, jobs, social events, relatives, emergencies etc. From the time we wake up till bedtime we are busy and sometimes the busyness does not translate to results that are connected to our life goals. We find ourselves caught between too many things seeking our time yet we are trying to recover our lost years. Solitude offers an escape from these pressing matters so as to concentrate on the important ones. It gives us an opportunity to concentrate and invest quality time into fulfilling our life's purpose.

We play several roles in our lives and each role demands our attention. So with each clamoring for more attention, we become overwhelmed. These are competing deadlines, urgent and important or unimportant matters but solitude is a means to gain some quiet and put order into our lives. It affords us the opportunity to de-clutter our lives and prioritize and put everything in its proper position.

For instance, Andrew is a Husband, Father, Finance Manager at his work, Head of the men's fellowship in his church and a doctoral student in the University. These roles demand his attention and without proper planning and prioritizing, he may neglect some and suffer the consequences. He may lose his marriage if his career gets more attention. Or he may lose his kids and suffer the pain of having delinquent children if he starves them of quality time.

Solitude is an opportunity for Andrew to withdraw from everything and everyone to re-assess his pursuits, re-define his goals and re-organize his life. It will help him to gain clarity and prioritize his activities. In addition, he could create a system whereby all areas of his life are well catered for and none is bereft of his attention.

Through Solitude, we can re-build our lives. Our lives are in constant need of improvement. Growth involves changing but most times we are too busy to incorporate the necessary changes that will enhance our performance. Solitude can provide an excellent opportunity to reflect inwards and eliminate our negative habits, patterns and attitudes.

I re-created myself through solitude. I changed my negative habits and imbibed new ones through the process of solitude. I changed my old value systems that were an impediment to my growth and copied new ones. I changed my mind-set and attitudes through the process of solitude.

SOLITUDE UNLOCKS OUR CREATIVITY

Great things are birthed through solitude. Nothing precious happens by chance, they are usually products of solitude. The time of solitude sparks our creativity and imagination and successful people take advantage of such moments to develop their works. Great artists, poets, musicians, painters of old were people who practiced solitude and produced great masterpieces during times of solitude.

There is power in a quiet mind, because our creative mind is activated during times of mental quietness. Many of the world's highest-paid people are able to tap into the vast resources of their creative minds to produce products and services that solve the problems of the masses.

I listened to the world's richest man, Bill Gates recently. He said that for many years, starting from his youthful days, he had practiced solitude. He usually took two weeks every year to be in solitude. No wonder he received and developed ideas that has changed the lives of humans and made him the world's richest man in the process. Great things are birthed through solitude.

Michelangelo di Lodovico Buonarroti Simoni, is an Italian sculptor, painter, architect and poet who was considered to be the greatest living artist during his lifetime and one of the greatest artists of all time. Michelangelo's works of painting, sculpture, and architecture rank among the most famous in existence. Some of his masterpieces include *David, Moses, Pietà* and the Sistine Chapel ceiling painting. When I visited the St. Basilica in the Vatican City where some of his works are preserved, I learnt he spent months to years in solitude to create his masterpieces. According to his biography he was by nature a solitary and melancholy person who withdrew himself from the company of men. His works of art could only have been produced in solitude, they are works of grandeur.

Great books are works of solitude. Most writers often go into solitude so as to receive more inspiration, and envision better. Through solitude, I have written three hundred books and numerous articles. No great thing can be produced with all the noise and distractions going on in our lives.

Jesus practiced solitude too. Before the commencement of his ministry, he was in the wilderness in solitude for forty days. "Then *Jesus was led by the Spirit into the wilderness to be tempted by the devil. After fasting forty days and forty nights, He was hungry.*"(Mathew 4:1-2 NIV).

And during the time of his ministry, he frequently departed to the mountains and spent entire nights alone in solitude.

One of those days Jesus went out to a mountainside to pray, and spent the night praying to God .When morning came, he called his disciples to him and chose twelve of them, whom he also designated apostles.
LUKE 6:12-13 NIV

Jesus practiced solitude before taking major decisions. He spent an entire night alone in prayers and communication with God and when he returned, he chose the twelve apostles.

Many scientists and inventors were people of solitude. Most of their inventions were discovered during times of solitude in their laboratories. Examples include Albert Einstein, George Washington Carver, and Thomas Edison etc.

HOW I PRACTISE SOLITUDE

To practice Solitude effectively, I engage the following:

1. Complete separation

Solitude is separation from every form of distraction in order to be alone. I go into solitude alone. You are not in solitude if you are not alone. So if you have the company of your phone, TV or social media, you are not in solitude. So find a place where you can be alone and undisturbed and get rid of all gadgets that will distract you.

2. Raw materials

You need raw materials to convert into final products. Solitude is not a time to be passive. Some view solitude as a time of quietness so as to meditate and reflect on life matters. My practice of solitude is different. Before I go into solitude, I decide on the goal to achieve. Then I go in with the materials that I need to study or work on to achieve that goal. Then I stay in solitude with time and my raw materials and convert them into finished products.

For example, I may decide to develop my money skills, so I get all the materials on finances which may include books, audio teachings, CD etc. Then alone with time and the materials, I study and research till I get the knowledge I want and sharpen my money skills.

Oftentimes as a pastor, I desire to know God better and develop his attributes into my life. So I embark on solitude with my bible, Concordances, and CDs. I spend time to fellowship with God, praying and having conversations with him. Then I study God, his nature, character and attributes. I study His attitudes and reactions in certain situations. Then I reflect on ways to emulate and act like him when faced with similar circumstances. I transform my knowledge of God's character into tangible products in my personal life.

Other times, I go into solitude with the aim of converting my ideas into written works. So I write books and articles. Through the practice of solitude, I have written and published over 300 books in Russian language. So solitude is about you alone with time and the raw materials you wish to convert into final products.

PRODUCTS OF SOLITUDE

Solitude is an opportunity to do many things, some of which include the following.

Self-Discovery

Solitude affords us a great opportunity to reflect inwards and discover who we are and what our life's purpose is. So many people do not know who they are and why they are here. They are not aware of their talents and skills which could be a pointer to their purpose. But in solitude you can do self-analysis and unravel your deepest desires and passions. By asking certain questions and endeavoring to answer them, you can discover yourself. Solitude enables you to discover your strengths and weaknesses too.

To discover yourself, during your solitude, study books and listen to materials on the subject and by prayer and deep reflection you will discover who you are and why you are here.

Some of my mentees have engaged solitude to discover their purpose in life. A lot of them were confused as to their calling, because they found themselves pursuing goals and careers mapped out for them by their parents and teachers. They didn't realize it was their responsibility to discover God's plan for their lives. After listening to me, some went into solitude with my book *WHO AM I? WHY AM I HERE?* and gained clarity on the real purpose of their existence on earth.

Self-Development

Solitude is an excellent opportunity to develop, enrich and add value to our lives by sharpening our in-born talents and acquiring new skills. Our talents need to be developed in order to be useful to us and to others. In addition they need to be sharpened to make them commercially viable. Similarly, to become relevant in our rapidly changing society, we need to acquire new skills or upgrade existing ones. Through solitude, we can develop skills indispensable to the fulfillment of our divine purpose.

For example, if you are a painter, during solitude you can improve and advance your painting skills. The same goes for any talent you want to enhance or any skill you want to grow. One of my members decided to go into solitude to hone his typing skills. He was very slow at typing on the PC and slow speed impacted his studies negatively. Due to his slow speed, assignments took him a longer time to submit and he could not take notes on his computer. After listening to me teach on the power of solitude, he decided to attack his typing challenge more aggressively. He went into solitude for two days and downloaded some typing software. By the time he emerged from solitude forty-eight hours later, he was typing like a pro.

There was another church member who had a passion for music and wanted to learn to play the keyboard. But he was a very busy man, working full time to take care of his family. He decided to take online lessons and practice solitude during the weekends. In less than three months, he was playing during church services. He had sharpened the skill of playing the keyboard and was very excited about it.

Solitude is a good avenue to evaluate our habits, patterns, attitudes and value systems in order to discard the wrong ones and imbibe the right. Since we can reflect inwards deeply during solitude, we can assess our habits and attitudes that are detrimental to our purpose and the achievement of our goals. And devise ways to get rid of them.

For instance, I was very timid and shy. So I went to work on myself to develop self-confidence because of its importance towards fulfilling my purpose. I got rid of my shyness and became so confident that people find it hard to believe that I was ever timid and fearful.

I have also used the period of solitude to develop the fruits of the Holy Spirit in my life. I studied Jesus and the way he lived while on earth and tried to copy his character traits by imitating him. I have also studied some great and successful men in history and copied certain habits and patterns that made them successful in their endeavors.

You can use the period of solitude to do the same. Study your heroes and mentors and copy the habits you admire in their lives and make them yours. Jesus should be your most important hero to emulate.

Spiritual Development

Solitude is a wonderful way to advance your relationship with God. It will enable you to develop greater intimacy with Jesus and the Holy Spirit. Through solitude, you can learn more about God and become a friend of God. You can also learn to hear his voice better and discover his plans for your life. Because you are quiet, you can hear his voice clearly and know what decision to take and what direction to go.

Every Christian needs to practice solitude just to be alone with God and enjoy his presence and build a deeper relationship with him. The deeper your relationship, the easier it will be to know his will and his next agenda for you. There will be no need to seek direction from others including pastors. When you practice solitude, you will learn to be led by his Spirit. *"For as many as are led by the Spirit of God, they are the sons of God"* (Romans 8:14 NIV)

Through solitude, you can increase your knowledge of God's word by in-depth study of the bible, Concordances, Greek and Hebrew study tools, books written by men of God and through listening to sermons.

Pursuit of Our Goals

Through solitude you can pursue your goals and visions in life. Having discovered your purpose, you can aim to fulfill it by developing all the skills you need to attain your goals during the time of solitude. For instance, if your purpose is to be an entrepreneur, you can enhance your skills while in solitude by reading and researching on your field of interest, learning from predecessors and contemporaries in the field. During solitude, you can envision, plan, project and develop your strategies. The time of solitude is an opportunity to hone your skills and be prepared to undertake the challenges out there.

When I discovered that God wanted me to be a pastor, I took out time to prepare myself. I practiced solitude, fasted, prayed and studied for several months before I stepped out. Some people do not deem it vital to prepare themselves for their assignments. They step out unprepared, no wonder many of their ventures fail. The bible says in the book of Proverbs;

> *By wisdom a house is built, And by understanding it is established.*
> PROVERBS 24:3 NIV

This means that the process of preparation is compulsory to the success of any project. With strong and adequate preparation the chances of failure are minimized to a large extent.

Before Jesus embarked on his ministry, he spent forty days of solitude in the wilderness getting ready. He was in fasting and prayers preparing himself for his assignment.

Although the son of God, he had to prepare himself using solitude. No wonder he completed his ministry successfully.

The preparation process using solitude is important for the success of our goals and visions. Solitude affords us the opportunity to reflect on our lives and work on our life's goals and purpose.

ADVANTAGES OF SOLITUDE

Focus and concentration

The time of solitude eliminates distractions from our life and our mind. Without distractions we are able to concentrate better and fully on the goal before us. With increased focus and concentration, we can invest more value into every hour of solitude and produce more goods or services.

Bulk time

During solitude, time killers and wasters are completely removed and we have 24 hours of the day at our disposal. It delivers bulk time into our hands to invest into our goals and visions. Depending on the number of days of your solitude, you can have 72 hours, 168 hours etc available to you. Thus it allows us to maximize our time.

Speed

Speed is a very important factor in regaining our lost years. Since it is a race against time, it is imperative to move at a faster speed. Because when there is maximum focus and concentration, speed is increased immensely leading to more products. During solitude, I write more books and more articles than when I am at home. You can achieve your goals faster when you practice solitude. As an IT developer, you can write more codes during solitude than when you have TV, friends or family around you. A pianist who goes into solitude for three days will master certain skills faster than another pianist who practices two hours every day.

Creativity

Times of solitude provide the quiet atmosphere which allows our creative mind to come into play and produce greater results. Times of solitude unlock our creativity and expose our mind to more inspiration leading to higher quality of output.

SOLITUDE WITH FOCUS, SPEED AND INTENSITY

Although we have seen the advantages of solitude, in reclaiming our lost years, we cannot practice solitude like others would. We cannot practice solitude at the same rate as others who are not competing against time. Rather our approach to the solitude has to be different.

In order to redeem your lost years and fulfill your divine purpose, you must practice solitude with Focus, Speed and Intensity. This means Solitude is mandatory and the frequency is high. So it is not optional and does not depend on when conditions are conducive.

Therefore, you need to practice solitude with a high degree of energy, enthusiasm and passion. It must be practiced with rapidity and result orientation. It must be practiced with a lot of focus and concentration.

Take every opportunity to practice solitude. And during your solitude, ensure you are focused on the products you want to create. Avoid daydreaming during solitude and work with speed. Set goals for your times of solitude and pursue your goals with intensity.

Unless solitude is practiced with Focus, Speed and Intensity, it will not produce maximum results.

CONCLUSION

In this chapter, you been introduced to a practice that will enable you produce more results than you have ever dreamed of. It is pertinent to put it into practice starting immediately. Set out times when you can practice solitude either every week or month. And invest that time into achieving your goals.

In the next and final chapter, we will look into one more principle that will help you regain your lost years. This principle is somewhat different from others yet very powerful.

THE GOLDEN NUGGETS

- Solitude is a time of complete separation or seclusion to be alone.

- Solitude offers a great opportunity to harness the entire 24 hours of the day to oneself.

- Solitude is a time to bring order into our lives.

- Solitude unlocks our creativity and enables us gain more inspiration.

- Great things arc birthed through solitude.

- During solitude, there are no distractions and our focus, concentration and speed are increased.

- Our goals and divine purpose can be pursued during times of solitude

- Solitude is a place of self-discovery and development.

- Great people including Jesus, practiced solitude regularly.

- Solitude, practiced with Focus, Speed and Intensity is a great tool to regain our lost years.

CHAPTER 13

MAXIMIZE OTHERS

In the previous chapters, we dealt with principles that will help you regain your lost years through your personal efforts. But in this chapter, the focus will be different. Instead of regaining your lost years through your personal efforts, you will learn to do so through other people.

In the beginning of this book, we learnt that successful people use not only their time but have found ways to use the time of others. They use people's time in exchange for some financial remuneration. In other words, they hire people to work for them.

When you employ people to work for you and help you accomplish your goals, you have multiplied your efforts and have gained time. Therefore to regain your lost years it is imperative to find ways of engaging other people's time. Thus it is not smart to work alone, rather find people who can work with you and together you will achieve more in less time.

Surround yourself with the best people you can find, delegate authority, and don't interfere as long as the policy you've decided upon is being carried out.

RONALD REAGAN

The goal of this book is not to teach you the importance of hiring people rather it is to teach you how to maximize their time and their potentials in order to regain your lost years. So in this chapter, you will learn how to maximize the time and efforts of your staff or employees.

MAXIMIZE THE POTENTIALS IN OTHERS

Maximize, according to the Merriam-Webster's Learner's Dictionary means to make as high or great as possible; to increase something to the maximum. It also means to use in a way that will get best results.

Therefore to maximize others means to make others as great as possible, increase their capacity to the maximum and to use them in a way that will yield the best results. It means to find people who are able to do what you do, teach and coach them to reach their highest potentials, engage their services then pay for their time.

In order to reclaim your lost years you need to hire people who have the needed potentials and train them. Teach them to fine tune their skills and develop their potentials to the maximum. Teach them to maximize their time by working with speed, focus and intensity. Train them to imbibe your work ethics and to produce the same quality of work. Then afterwards, delegate your goals, tasks and assignments to them. Because you have optimized their potentials, they will be your replica, and in this way, you have been able to multiply yourself and your time. Great leaders multiply themselves by delegation.

So in order to optimize the potentials of your staff, and regain your lost time, you have to train them both on the responsibilities and tasks to handle and also teach them to work with speed, focus and intensity. When projects and assignments are performed with speed, focus and intensity, a lot will be accomplished within a shorter time.

Jesus Christ was a great leader who according to the scriptures maximized the potentials of others in an attempt to fulfill his divine purpose. According to the book of Matthew, at the inception of his ministry, he appointed twelve disciples. These were ordinary men who did not know much about religion. Apart from Luke, the medical doctor and Matthew, the tax collector, the rest were mainly fishermen who did not have any formal education. They were neither priests nor teachers of the law, popularly called the Pharisees.

But over the three years of his ministry, Jesus trained and coached them. When he spoke parables to the multitudes, he explained the meaning to his twelve disciples. And when he healed the sick or casted out demons, he explained the secret behind whatever he did to them. Sometimes, he sent them out on evangelism to practice what they learnt. They travelled from city to city, preaching the gospel, healing the sick and casting out devils and returned with reports of their exploits.

After his death and resurrection, just before Jesus ascended to heaven, he commanded them saying: *"Therefore go and make disciples of all nations, baptizing them in the name of the Father and of the Son and of the Holy Spirit, and teaching them to obey everything I have commanded you. And surely I am with you always, to the very end of the age."* (Matthew 28:19-20 NIV)

He had completed their training and was delegating a divine assignment to them. On the day of Pentecost, Peter, a fisherman preached and over three thousand people were converted to Christianity. They couldn't have been able to accomplish their assignment if Jesus had not trained and maximized their potentials.

> *With many other words he warned them; and*
> *he pleaded with them, "Save yourselves from*
> *this corrupt generation." Those who accepted his*
> *message were baptized, and about three thousand*
> *were added to their number that day.*
> ACTS 2:40-41 NIV

They continued preaching and doing many exploits in the name of Jesus that people were amazed at their boldness and courage. However they realized that they were disciples of Jesus and were simply acting like their master and coach.

> *When they saw the courage of Peter and John and*
> *realized that they were unschooled, ordinary men,*
> *they were astonished and they took note that these*
> *men had been with Jesus.*
> ACTS 4:13 NIV

Jesus multiplied himself and his time by investing in the lives of his disciples and optimizing their potentials. Although he lived on earth for about thirty-three years, his legacy has been passed down generations because he maximized the potentials of a few men.

So the emphasis is not about delegation but to delegate to people whose potentials have been maximized. So in order to optimize the potentials of your staff, and regain your lost time, you have to train them both on the responsibilities and tasks to handle and to work with speed, focus and intensity. When projects and assignments are performed with these three qualities, more will be accomplished within a shorter time.

DELEGATE

The best executive is the one who has sense enough to pick good men to do what he wants done, and self-restraint enough to keep from meddling with them while they do it.
THEODORE ROOSEVELT

Personally, I delegate my assignments to people whom I have trained and empowered. I do not simply train them to perform my assignments but I train them on my work ethics as well. I train them to work with speed, focus and intensity in order to maximize their time. So my staff work like me. They work fast and smart and are able to get much done within a shorter amount of time. In this way, I reclaim my lost years.

In the city of Kyiv Ukraine, where I pastor, I have been able to multiply and replicate myself in the lives of a lot of people. I raised leaders who have raised more leaders and are affecting more people than I possibly could reach.

For instance, there are pastors whom I trained and sent out to start their own churches. They grew their churches and they gave birth to ten or twenty more churches. And the baby churches are giving birth to more and more churches too. Presently, we have over 450 autonomous churches in Ukraine. This is the power of maximizing the potentials of others.

In addition to empowering my members to start their own churches, I have raised leaders who are affecting their world; with followership in thousands yet they are neither pastors nor church leaders. They have organizations and movements through which they are doing exploits by changing the lives of people and adding value to them. These leaders are not merely influencing millions, but they are also raising great leaders as well. Some are rehabilitating alcoholics, drug addicts and prostitutes while others are impacting the youths in high schools and universities. Some are involved in the banking system while some are working with the paralegal. Lives are being changed and the nation of Ukraine is impacted positively.

All these are not possible for a single leader to accomplish but by maximizing others, I have been able to multiply myself and my time to reach more people and do more exploits for the kingdom of God.

ENGAGE PROFESSIONALS

Besides training and maximizing people in order to delegate your tasks and responsibilities to them, you can find professionals and delegate to them as well. In other words, you can employ the services of professionals in a field to get your job done thereby saving your time and investing it into some other task.

In some western countries, people need to prepare their tax returns for the year. While there are professional accountants who can do the job easily and allow you focus on other tasks, some people prefer to do it by themselves in order to save the money. This is a scenario where you need to calculate the value of the time you invested into the exercise and compare it with the accountant's fees. But if you want to regain your lost years, you will engage a professional and invest your time into fulfilling your goals.

Some people are fond of engaging in tasks that they are not proficient in simply to save small amounts of money.

Personally, I prefer to engage the services of professionals and pay their fees because my time is much more valuable than their fees. After my wife and I got married, I asked her to stop cooking instead let us contract it out to someone who will cook and clean the house. But she refused, she felt it was her wifely duty to cook and clean. And being a Nigerian, it was the role of a wife to cook for her husband and her kids. My wife is an intelligent and smart lady, an Engineer by profession. I could not bear the fact that marrying me had reduced her to spending valuable hours of her life in the kitchen, just to cook my meals, a task that any cook could do.

It took several years to convince her. We were not rich at that time and we could barely afford the fees, so we combined resources with another couple and engaged the services of a lady who came in to cook and clean twice a week.

Thus my wife was liberated from spending hours in the kitchen and in house chores and invested the time into adding value to her life. She grew so much in spiritual matters that she is presently the resident pastor of our twenty-five thousand member church in Kyiv Ukraine. By engaging the services of professionals, she was able to invest her time into more worthwhile ventures and is fulfilling God's purpose for her life.

This is the reason why I do not drive myself but I employ a driver to do so. My time is so precious and valuable that I cannot waste it on a mundane task like driving. What I make in less than three hours is more than enough to pay a driver for a full month. So why waste my time?

So in reclaiming your lost years, enlist the services of professionals you can afford and invest your time into adding value to your life and fulfilling God's plan and purpose for your life.

MAXIMIZE PEOPLE'S RESOURCES

To regain your lost time, learn to maximize the resources of others. These may include their time, money, skills or knowledge.

As an entrepreneur, you can leverage on people's money if your goal is to recover your lost years financially. It is a wise idea to take a loan from the bank in order to grow your business and increase your profit. A loan is a way of maximizing other people's money to grow your business faster.

Some Christians feel that it is wrong to borrow money, but a loan is a good thing if the aim is to invest it to grow your business. A bad loan is when you borrow money to solve personal problems or when it is not invested in a profitable enterprise. Some borrow money to buy a car; that is a bad loan. Others borrow money to pay hospital bills; that is also a bad loan. A loan must be invested and it must yield interest in excess of the interest being charged on it. The difference between both becomes your profit. Never take a loan that does not yield profit to you.

Successful business owners understand the advantage of using other people's money to make profit for themselves. That is why they prefer to take a loan from the bank to grow their businesses but invest their own money elsewhere. Even banks use people's funds to enrich themselves and pay a stipend to them as interest.

In regaining your lost years, it is expedient to utilize professional advice and consultancy where need be. We cannot be masters in all fields of life. There are individuals who experts in their field and their wealth of knowledge and experience can get you further faster. For instance, there are consultants in almost every field of endeavor who can jump start your career or business and take it to new heights. Hiring a consultant may seem to be a waste of resources, but in the long run, it isn't.

It is noteworthy that professional athletes invest their resources to hire a good coach or trainer. They understand the importance of having professional guidance to maximize their skills and sharpen their talents.

Usain Bolt, the fastest man in the world is an example of how professional guidance can affect the realization of one's goals and dreams. Coach Glen Mills from Jamaica is the secret behind the success of Usain Bolt.

After a disappointing showing at the Athens Olympics, Bolt sought out Glen Mills as the man who might enable him to finally fulfill his dreams. Although naturally gifted, Glen Mills recognized Bolt's poor mechanics which resulted in injuries and poor performances. He developed a two year project of pulling apart the sprinter's technique, painstakingly breaking his bad habits, and developed his strength and improved his sprint techniques thereby transforming him into the fastest man in the world.

Coach Glen Mills who is a technical coach in the sprints and sprinting technique is one of the main reasons for Usain Bolt's domination in the sport of track and field. Without the professional help from Coach Mills, the name Usain Bolt may not have become a household name.

To reclaim your lost years, find professionals in your field and maximize their wisdom, knowledge and wealth of experience.

THE GOLDEN NUGGETS

- In order to reclaim our lost years, it is important to utilize other people's potentials.

- Great leaders excel in maximizing the potentials of their followers.

- Jesus was a great leader who fulfilled his purpose by maximizing the potentials of his followers.

- The art of delegation is a way of getting more done within a shorter time.

- Delegate to trained and maximized personnel who will work with focus, speed and intensity.

- Delegate tasks to professionals and specialists in the field.

- The importance of professional guidance in the fulfillment of our purpose cannot be under-estimated.

- Maximize the resources of others e.g. their time, money, skills and wealth of knowledge.

EPILOGUE

Congratulations for coming to the end of this book! I know that it has been a life transforming journey for you. You have seen that regaining your lost years is not only a possibility but I trust that you have actually started the process by practicing all you have been learning.

We have seen that a wrong attitude to time is one of the major reasons why people mismanage time. Time is our greatest earthly possession and it has to be valued and protected from time killers. We have seen several habits that are time killers but the advent of social media has worsened the situation. Hours are spent on social media without any resultant positive results. It is absolutely important to put a restriction on the amount of time spent on social media, TV, social activities etc.

You have been given time-proven principles that will help you to reclaim your lost years. These principles were employed by individuals and nations and will produce the same results in your life if you would commit to practicing them.

As reiterated many times, the key to regaining your lost years is investing maximum value into every second and hour of the day. This will ensure that you produce more results within each hour unlike before.

Amongst the principles discussed in this book, the single and most important one that will restore your lost years is Intensity. The practice of being intense towards any task will bring about speedy results. The habit of intensity was responsible for the success of the Asian tigers in developing their economy from third world nation to first world within a few decades.

But to accelerate the process of reclaiming your lost years, it is imperative to combine more qualities together rather than intensity alone. There are three qualities when combined produce the highest benefits; they are Speed, Focus and Intensity.

Whatever you wish to produce, either value to your life or others, goods or services, the inclusion of these three qualities will triple your speed and increase your results. Every activity that is targeted towards the attainment of your goals must be done with Speed, Focus and Intensity. Whether it involves work, solitude, self-education, it should be engaged in with speed, focus and intensity in order to yield maximum results. These keys will help you to regain your lost years.

So as earlier said, you hold in your hands, the keys and strategies that will enable you regain your lost years. The rest depends on you. I would like to remind you once again on how to get the best out of this book. These were discussed in detail at the beginning of the book.

To ensure that you redeem your lost years, go back and read this book again. Read it out loud and underline the important points and ideas found in the book. Then re-read the underlined points and begin immediately to practice what you learnt. Secondly pay attention to the nuggets and exercises discussed in the conclusion section. Put them to practice immediately.

These will ensure that this book is not just one more book amongst your list rather, a book that transformed your life and helped you to regain your lost years.

REFERENCES

Chapter 1 • Can I Regain My Lost Years?

1. Pewtrust.org, "The Impact of the September 2008 Economic Collapse", April 28, 2010, *http://www.pewtrusts.org/en/research-and-analysis/reports/2010/04/28/the-impact-of-the-september-2008-economic-collapse* (accessed November 9, 2016).

2. "The effects of Hurricane Katrina on New Orleans Economy", Monthly Labour Review, June 2007, *http://www.bls.gov/opub/mlr/2007/06/art1full.pdf* (accessed November 9, 2016).

3. USlegal.com, "Profiles of famous/newsworthy bankruptcies", *https://bankruptcy.uslegal.com/profilesfamousbankruptcies/walt-disney/* (accessed November 9, 2016).

4. Biography.com, "Colonel Harland Sanders Biography", *http://www.biography.com/people/colonel-harland-sanders-12353545* (accessed November 9, 2016).

Chapter 2 • Time, Our Greatest Treasure

1. Kane L. June 26, 2014, "9 things rich people do and don't do everyday", *http://www.businessinsider.com/rich-people-daily-habits-2014-6* (accessed November 12, 2016).

Chapter 5 • Learn To Say "No"

1. Go-globe.com, "Social Media Addiction- Statistics and Trends", *http://www.go-globe.com/blog/social-media-addiction/* (accessed, November 10, 2016).

2. Wallace K., (2015, November 3), "Teens spend a 'mind-boggling' 9 hours a day using media, report says", *http://www.cnn.com/2015/11/03/health/teens-tweens-media-screen-use-report/* (accessed, November 10, 2016).

Chapter 7 • Be Intense

1. Nytimes.com, (2015, October 10), "The Asian Advantage", *http://www.nytimes.com/2015/10/11/opinion/sunday/the-asian-advantage.html?_r=1* (accessed , November 2016).

2. Todayonline.com, "Singapore world's most expensive city third year row says eiu report", a *http://www.todayonline.com/singapore/singapore-worlds-most-expensive-city-third-year-row-says-eiu-report* (accessed November 22, 2016).

3. Topuniversities.com, "Faculty rankings arts and humanities, humanities, *http://www.topuniversities.com/university-rankings/faculty-rankings/arts-and-humanities/2015* (accessed November 22, 2016).

4. Newshub.nus.edu.sg, "NUS attains 11th spot in the Financial Times Executive MBA 2009 rankings", October 19th 2009, *http://newshub.nus.edu.sg/headlines/1009/ranking_19Oct09.php,* (accessed November 22, 2016).

5. Pwc.com, "Cities of opportunities" *http://www.pwc.com/us/en/cities-of-opportunity/2014/assets/cities-of-opportunity-2014.pdf,* (accessed November 22, 2016).

6. Investopedia.com, "The world's Top 10 economies",
    July18, 2016, *http://www.investopedia.com/
    articles/investing/022415/worlds-top-10-
    economies.asp*, (accessed November 22, 2016).

7. Kleiner, JüRgen (2001). Korea, **A Century of Change.**
    ISBN 978-981-02-4657-0. *https://books.google.
    com/books?id=nTCC2ZheFuoC&pg=PA254&lpg
    =PA254&dq=han+river+miracle&q=han+river+
    miracle&hl=en#v=snippet&q=han%20river%20
    miracle&f=false* (Accessed November 22, 2016).

Chapter 10 • Conversion Through Hard Work

1. **Forbes.com, "The Sleep Habits of Highly Successful
    People"** November 13, 2015, *http://www.forbes.com/
    sites/alicegwalton/2015/11/13/the-sleep-habits-of-
    highly-successful-people-infographic/#6c9c79fb386f*,
    (accessed November 22, 2016).

INFORMATION ABOUT THE EMBASSY OF GOD CHURCH AND PASTOR SUNDAY ADELAJA

Pastor Sunday Adelaja — The only black man in the world that leads a congregation of mostly Caucasians in 50 countries. Below are some facts about Pastor Sunday's life and ministry.

- Pastor Sunday is the pastor of the largest Evangelical Church in Europe with a population of 99,9% white Europeans in Kiev Ukraine.
- His ministry has charity units that feed over 5000 people on a daily basis.
- Through his ministry over 30 thousand people have been delivered from drug and alcohol addictions.
- He helped raise over 200 millionaires in US dollars in his church, most of whom were former drug/ alcohol addicts and societal outcasts.
- He has raised a global movement that is influencing over 70million people around the globe.
- Branches of his church are in over 50 countries.
- He has spoken in different nations of the world on National Transformation.
- Pastor Sunday is one of the few, if not the only African, who has ever spoken in the US senate.
- Pastor Sunday is one of the few African pastors who has spoken on the floor of the UN.
- He has addressed the Japanese Members of parliament.
- He has spoken in the Knesset to members of Israeli parliament. The list goes on and on.
- His ministry has over 500 hundred government officials holding different government positions in Ukraine.
- He has written and published over 300 books and recorded thousands of messages.

THE EMBASSY OF GOD CHURCH

There are more than 300 rehabilitation centers for alcohol and drug addicts which have been operational in Ukraine and Europe since 1994.

More than 20,000 people recovered from their addictions, and became normal members of the society. Thanks to the rehabilitation centers opened by the church.

There are homes for abandoned street children operated by the church which have successfully reunited more than 5,000 children with their families.

The Embassy of God Church is involved in many social projects that are directed at maintaining family values, active civil involvement and individual fulfillment of church members.

Many former members of mafia organizations and criminals have become devout Christians through the missionary work of the Embassy of God Church.

The church's hot-line has counseled over a 200,000 people.

Right now there are over 25,000 members in the Embassy of God Church Kyiv, Ukraine.

BIOGRAPHY OF PASTOR SUNDAY ADELAJA

Pastor Sunday Adelaja is the Founder and Senior Pastor of The Embassy of the Blessed Kingdom of God for All Nations Church in Kyiv, Ukraine.

He is a Nigerian-born leader with an apostolic gift for the twenty-first century. In his mid thirties Pastor Sunday had already proven to be one of the world's most dynamic communicators and church planters and is regarded as the most successful pastor in Europe with over 25,000 members as well as daughter and satellite churches in over 50 countries worldwide.

The congregation includes members from all spheres of society, from former drug and alcohol addicts, to politicians and millionaires. It's high percentage of white Europeans (99%), also indicates that boundaries of racial prejudice have been surpassed. In the same country where Pastor Sunday was called "chocolate rabbit" and several attempts have been made to deport him, thousands join hands and support his mission to see Ukraine and the whole world affected and saved by the gospel of the Kingdom. Pastor Sunday is recognized as an unusually gifted teacher of the Word of God, with an extraordinary operation in the gifts of the Spirit, especially the word of knowledge. He receives numerous speaking invitations to several countries in all continents of the world yearly, as well as invitations to meetings with heads of States and other Politicians.

Pastor Sunday's influence in the areas of church growth, prayer and evangellsm has been noted by Charisma Magazine, Ministries Today and many other Christian periodicals. The secular world media, such as the Wall Street Journal, Forbes, Washington Post, Reuters, Associated Press, CNN, BBC and German, Dutch and French national television have all widely reported on him. The Wall Street Journal called him "A Man with a Mission" set out to save Kyiv. The Ukrainian President Yushenko acknowledged his strong involvement in the Orange revolution for democracy in Ukraine. Former Mayor of New York City Rudolph Giuliani stated: *"Sunday, God bless you in your important mission. When I next come to Ukraine I would like to be at your church"*.

In August 2007 by invitation from the employees of the UN, Pastor Sunday Adelaja was invited as a speaker for three sessions. It was the first time in the history of the UN that a pastor speaks in the main hall of the UN. There were 500 organizations and missions from different parts of the world and leaders from 30 countries that participated in these sessions. From then on, the Embassy of God started its preparation to enter the UN and become a member of this organization.

Pastor Sunday's passion for National Transformation has driven him to maximally spread the word of God. He has written and published over 200 books of which some have been translated to English, German, Chinese, Arabic and Dutch. Also, thousands of sermons have been recorded. He organizes annual pastors leadership seminars where over 1,000 ministers regularly attend, studying the topic 'Pastoring without Tears'. His passion is to ignite these ministers with fire and power to transform their cities and countries.

Every year Pastor Sunday organizes Pastor's Seminars that take place in the church. He is also the main speaker there. During this time more than 1,000 Ministers learn how to be a pastor without tears, and learn the keys of achieving success. Also, every year Pastor Sunday organizes a summer and winter fast which aims at equipping Ministers with fire and power to change their cities and countries.

Nowadays, the apostolic ministry of Pastor Sunday has gone far beyond the boundaries of Ukraine, making him a desirable speaker and a Pastor to Pastors in many nations of the world. To date, he has visited over 50 countries.

Pastor Sunday is happily married to his "Princess" Abosede, and they are blessed with three children: Perez, Zoe and Pearl.

Below is the link to a photo gallery of Pastor Sunday and other likeminded individuals who have also positively impacted their nations:

http://www.godembassy.com/media/photo/view-album/3.html

FOLLOW
SUNDAY ADELAJA
ON SOCIAL MEDIA

Subscribe And Read Pastor Sunday's Blog:
www.sundayadelajablog.com

Follow these links and listen to over 200
of Pastor Sunday's Messages free of charge:
http://sundayadelajablog.com/content/

Follow Pastor Sunday on Twitter:
www.twitter.com/official_pastor

Join Pastor Sunday's Facebook page to stay in touch:
www.facebook.com/pastor.sunday.adelaja

Visit our websites for more information
about Pastor Sunday's ministry:
http://www.godembassy.com
http://www.pastorsunday.com
http://sundayadelaja.de

CONTACT

FOR DISTRIBUTION OR TO ORDER
BULK COPIES OF THIS BOOK,
PLEASE CONTACT US:

USA
CORNERSTONE PUBLISHING
info@thecornerstonepublishers.com
+1 (516) 547-4999
www.thecornerstonepublishers.com

AFRICA
Sunday Adelaja Media Ltd.
E-mail: btawolana@hotmail.com
+2348187518530, +2348097721451, +2348034093699

LONDON, UK
Pastor Abraham Great
abrahamagreat@gmail.com
+447711399828, +44-1908538141

KIEV, UKRAINE
pa@godembassy.org
Mobile: +380674401958

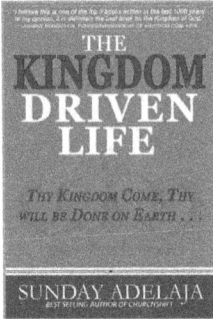

The Kingdom Driven Life:
Thy Kingdom Come, Thy Will be
Done on Earth
(Best seller)

Myles Munroe:
... Finding Answers To Why Good
People Die Tragic And Early Deaths

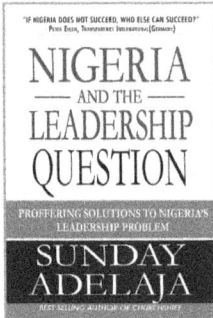

Nigeria And
The Leadership Question:
Proffering Solutions To Nigeria's
Leadership Problem

Olorunwa (There Is Sunday):
Portrait Of Sunday Adelaja.
The Roads Of Life

Available on Amazon.com, Kindle and Okadabooks.com

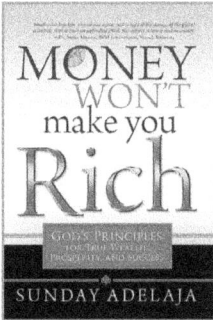

Money Won't Make You Rich:
God's Principles for True Wealth,
Prosperity, and Success

Who Am I? Why Am I here?:
How to discover your purpose and
calling in life

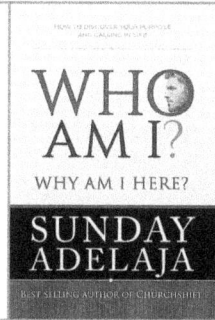

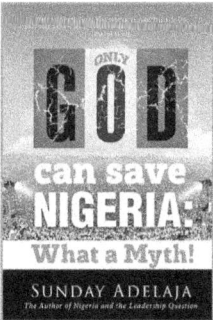

Only God Can Save Nigeria:
What a Myth?

Church Shift:
Revolutionizing Your Faith, Church,
and Life for the 21st Century

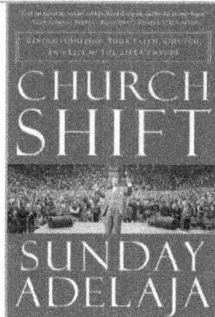

... and many more

www.ingramcontent.com/pod-product-compliance
Lightning Source LLC
Chambersburg PA
CBHW022126080426
42734CB00006B/247